PRISM

READING AND WRITING
TEACHER'S MANUAL

2

Carolyn Westbrook

Lida Baker

with
Wendy Asplin
Janet Gokay
Jeanne Lambert
Kate Adams

CAMBRIDGE
UNIVERSITY PRESS

CAMBRIDGE
UNIVERSITY PRESS

University Printing House, Cambridge CB2 8BS, United Kingdom

One Liberty Plaza, 20th Floor, New York, NY 10006, USA

477 Williamstown Road, Port Melbourne, VIC 3207, Australia

4843/24, 2nd Floor, Ansari Road, Daryaganj, Delhi – 110002, India

79 Anson Road, #06–04/06, Singapore 079906

Cambridge University Press is part of the University of Cambridge.

It furthers the University's mission by disseminating knowledge in the pursuit of education, learning and research at the highest international levels of excellence.

www.cambridge.org
Information on this title: www.cambridge.org/9781316625132

First published 2017
20 19 18 17 16 15 14 13 12 11 10 9 8 7 6 5 4 3 2 1

Printed in Malaysia by Vivar Printing

A catalogue record for this publication is available from the British Library

ISBN 978-1-316-62513-2 Teacher's Manual 2 Reading and Writing
ISBN 978-1-316-62431-9 Student's Book with Online Workbook 2 Reading and Writing

Cambridge University Press has no responsibility for the persistence or accuracy of URLs for external or third-party internet websites referred to in this publication, and does not guarantee that any content on such websites is, or will remain, accurate or appropriate. Information regarding prices, travel timetables, and other factual information given in this work is correct at the time of first printing but Cambridge University Press does not guarantee the accuracy of such information thereafter.

CONTENTS

SCOPE AND SEQUENCE

UNIT	WATCH AND LISTEN	READINGS	READING SKILLS	LANGUAGE DEVELOPMENT	
1 ANIMALS *Academic Disciplines* Ecology / Zoology	Great Egret and Dolphin Fishing Teamwork	1: Endangered species (factsheet) 2: Losing the Battle for Survival (article)	*Key Skill* Reading for main ideas *Additional Skills* Understanding key vocabulary Using your knowledge Reading for details Working out meaning Summarizing Making inferences Synthesizing	Academic verbs Comparative adjectives	
2 THE ENVIRONMENT *Academic Disciplines* Environmental Science / Natural Science	Colorado River, Grand Canyon, Yosemite	1: Our Changing Planet (web page) 2: The Causes and Effects of Deforestation (essay)	*Key Skill* Reading for details *Additional Skills* Understanding key vocabulary Predicting content using visuals Reading for main ideas Scanning to find information Identifying purpose Previewing Summarizing Making inferences Synthesizing	Academic vocabulary Environment collocations	
3 TRANSPORTATION *Academic Disciplines* Transportation Management / Urban Planning	The Jumbo Jet	1: Masdar: the Future of Cities? (case study) 2: A reading about traffic congestion (essay)	*Key Skill* Predicting content using visuals *Additional Skills* Understanding key vocabulary Reading for main ideas Reading for details Making inferences Synthesizing	Transportation collocations Synonyms for verbs	
4 CUSTOMS AND TRADITIONS *Academic Disciplines* Cultural Studies / Sociology	Halloween by the Numbers	1: Customs Around the World (article) 2: Nontraditional Weddings (article)	*Key Skill* Annotating *Additional Skills* Understanding key vocabulary Using your knowledge Reading for main ideas Reading for details Making inferences Previewing Synthesizing	Avoiding generalizations Adverbs of frequency Synonyms to avoid repetition	

CRITICAL THINKING	GRAMMAR FOR WRITING	WRITING	ON CAMPUS
Use a Venn diagram	Word order Combining sentences • *and* and *or* • *but* and *whereas* • *both* and *neither*	**_Academic Writing Skills_** Topic sentences **_Rhetorical Mode_** Comparison and contrast **_Writing Task_** Compare and contrast the two sharks in the diagram. (essay completion)	**_Research Skill_** Avoiding plagiarism
Use a cause-effect chart	Verbs of cause and effect *Because* and *because of*	**_Academic Writing Skills_** Paragraph unity Supporting sentences and details **_Rhetorical Mode_** Cause and effect **_Writing Task_** Describe the human causes of climate change and the effects that climate change will have on the planet. (essay completion)	**_Life Skill_** Choosing your courses
Identify and evaluate problems and solutions	Future real conditional *if ... not* and *unless*	**_Academic Writing Skill_** Writing a concluding sentence **_Rhetorical Mode_** Problem and solution **_Writing Task_** Discuss the advantages and disadvantages of two solutions to a city's traffic congestion problems. (essay completion)	**_Study Skill_** Creating idea maps
Analyze a text Evaluate and respond to an author's ideas	Paraphrasing	**_Academic Writing Skills_** Writing a summary and a personal response **_Rhetorical Mode_** Summary and response **_Writing Task_** Summarize and respond to Reading 2. Give your opinions about the changes in wedding traditions. (paragraphs)	**_Communications Skills_** Communicating with professors

UNIT	WATCH AND LISTEN	READINGS	READING SKILLS	LANGUAGE DEVELOPMENT	
5 HEALTH AND FITNESS _Academic Disciplines_ Medicine / Nutrition	Nutrition Labels	1: A reading about health and exercise (article) 2: Tackling Obesity (essay)	_Key Skill_ Making inferences _Additional Skills_ Understanding key vocabulary Predicting content using visuals Skimming Reading for main ideas Reading for details Using your knowledge Scanning to predict content Synthesizing	Verb and noun forms Health and fitness collocations	
6 DISCOVERY AND INVENTION _Academic Disciplines_ Industrial Design / Mechanical Engineering	China's Man-made River	1: The Magic of Mimicry (article) 2: The World of Tomorrow (article)	_Key Skill_ Scanning to find information _Additional Skills_ Understanding key vocabulary Using your knowledge Reading for main ideas Annotating Making inferences Reading for details Synthesizing	Making predictions with modals and adverbs of certainty Prefixes	
7 FASHION _Academic Disciplines_ Fashion Design / Retail Management	A Life Tailored Around Clothes	1: Is Fast Fashion Taking Over? (article) 2: Offshore Production (essay)	_Key Skills_ Distinguishing fact from opinion _Additional Skills_ Understanding key vocabulary Using your knowledge Reading for main ideas Reading for details Making inferences Skimming Scanning to find information Synthesizing	Vocabulary for the fashion business	
8 ECONOMICS _Academic Disciplines_ Business / Economics	The Stock Market Crash of 1929	1: How Should You Invest Your Money? (article) 2: Income and Expenditure, 1996-2014 (article)	_Key Skills_ Skimming _Additional Skills_ Understanding key vocabulary Using your knowledge Reading for main ideas Reading for details Making inferences Annotating Synthesizing	Nouns and adjectives for economics Nouns for economic trends	

CRITICAL THINKING	GRAMMAR FOR WRITING	WRITING	ON CAMPUS
Subdivide arguments	Stating opinions Stating a purpose	*Academic Writing Skills* Essay structure *Rhetorical Mode* Opinion *Writing Task* Should colleges and universities require students to take physical education classes? (essay)	*Study Skill* Avoiding procrastination
Use T-charts to brainstorm and organize ideas	Relative clauses Prepositional phrases with advantages and disadvantages	*Academic Writing Skill* Writing an introductory paragraph *Rhetorical Mode* Explanatory *Writing Task* Choose a new area of technology or invention and discuss its advantages and disadvantages. (essay)	*Study Skill* Annotating texts
Identify and strengthen arguments	Multiword prepositions	*Academic Writing Skills* Body paragraphs in argumentative essays Cohesion *Rhetorical Mode* Argumentative *Writing Task* The fashion industry is harmful to society and the environment. Do you agree or disagree? (essay)	*Research Skill* Using Internet sources
Understand and interpret line graphs	Describing graphs—noun phrases and verb phrases Prepositions and conjunctions Approximations	*Academic Writing Skill* Writing a concluding paragraph *Rhetorical Mode* Analysis *Writing Task* Describe the multiple-line graph showing home video revenue and explain the data. (essay)	*Life Skill* College applications

Prism is a five-level paired skills series for beginner- to advanced-level students of North American English. Its five Reading and Writing and five Listening and Speaking levels are designed to equip students with the language and skills to be successful both inside and outside of the college classroom.

Prism uses a fresh approach to Critical Thinking based on a full integration of Bloom's taxonomy to help students become well-rounded critical thinkers. The productive half of each unit begins with Critical Thinking. This section gives students the skills and tools they need to plan and prepare for success in their Speaking or Writing Task. Learners develop lower- and higher-order thinking skills, ranging from demonstrating knowledge and understanding to in-depth evaluation and analysis of content. Margin labels in the Critical Thinking sections highlight exercises that develop Bloom's concepts.

Prism focuses on the most relevant and important language for students of academic English based on comprehensive research. Key vocabulary is taken from the General Service List, the Academic Word List, and the Cambridge English Corpus. The grammar selected is also corpus-informed.

Prism goes beyond language and critical thinking skills to teach students how to be successful, engaged college students both inside and outside of the classroom. On Campus spreads at the end of each unit introduce students to communication, study, presentation, and life skills that will help them transition to life in North American community college and university programs.

Prism combines print and digital solutions for the modern student and program. Online workbooks give students additional graded language and skills practice. Video resources are available to students and teachers in the same platform. Presentation Plus gives teachers modern tools to enhance their students' learning environment in the classroom.

Prism provides assessment resources for the busy teacher. Photocopiable unit quizzes and answer keys are included in the Teacher's Manual, with downloadable PDF and Word versions available at Cambridge.org/prism and in the Resource tab of the Cambridge Learning Management System. Writing rubrics for grading Writing Tasks in the Student's Book and on the Unit Writing Quizzes are included in the Teacher's Manual.

SERIES LEVELS

Level	Description	CEFR Levels
Prism Intro	Beginner	A1
Prism 1	Low Intermediate	A2
Prism 2	Intermediate	B1
Prism 3	High Intermediate	B2
Prism 4	Advanced	C1

UNIT OPENER

Each unit opens with a striking two-page photo related to the topic, a Learning Objectives box, and an Activate Your Knowledge activity.

PURPOSE

- To introduce and generate interest in the unit topic with an engaging visual
- To set the learning objectives for the unit
- To make connections between students' background knowledge and the unit topic/ theme

TEACHING SUGGESTIONS

PHOTO SPREAD

Lead an open class discussion on the connection between the unit opener photo and topic. Start off with questions like:

- *What is the first thing you notice in the photographs?*
- *What do you think of when you look at the photo?*
- *How is the photo connected to the unit title?*

ACTIVATE YOUR KNOWLEDGE

After students work in pairs to discuss the questions, have volunteers share with the class answers to questions that generated the most discussion.

You can also use the exercise to practice fluency. Instruct students to answer the questions as quickly as possible without worrying about creating grammatically correct sentences. Keep time and do not allow students more than 15–60 seconds per answer, depending on level and complexity of the question. You can then focus on accuracy when volunteers share their answers with the class.

WATCH AND LISTEN

Each unit includes a short authentic video from a respected news source that is related to the unit topic, along with exercises for students to do before, during, and after watching. The video can be played in the classroom or watched outside of class by students via the Cambridge LMS.

Note: A glossary defines above-level or specialized words that appear in the video and are essential for students to understand the main ideas so that teachers do not have to spend time pre-teaching or explaining this vocabulary while viewing.

PURPOSE

- To create a varied and dynamic learning experience
- To generate further interest in and discussion of the unit topic
- To build background knowledge and ideas on the topic
- To develop and practice key skills in prediction, comprehension, and discussion
- To personalize and give opinions on a topic

TEACHING SUGGESTIONS

PREPARING TO WATCH

Have students work in pairs to complete the Activating Your Knowledge exercise. Then have volunteers share their answers. Alternatively, students can complete this section on their own, and then compare answers with their partners.

For a livelier class discussion, look at the visuals from the Predicting Content Using Visuals exercise as a class and answer the questions together.

WHILE WATCHING

Watch the video twice, once while students listen for main ideas and once while they listen for key details. After each viewing, facilitate a discussion of students' answers and clarify any confusion. If some students still have trouble with comprehension, suggest that they watch the video again at home or during a computer lab session.

DISCUSSION

Have students work in pairs or small groups to answer the discussion questions. Have students compare their answers with another pair or group. Then have volunteers share their answers with the class. If possible, expand on their answers by making connections between their answers and the video content. For example: *That's an interesting perspective. How is it similar to what the speaker in the video mentioned? How is it different?*

For writing practice, have students write responses to the questions for homework.

READING

The first half of each unit focuses on the receptive skill of reading. Each unit includes two reading passages that provide different angles, viewpoints, and/or genres related to the unit topic.

READING 1

Reading 1 includes a reading passage on an academic topic. It provides information on the unit topic, and it gives students exposure to and practice with language and reading skills while helping them begin to generate ideas for their Writing Task.

PREPARING TO READ

PURPOSE

- To prepare students to understand the content of the reading
- To introduce, review, and/or practice key pre-reading skills
- To introduce and build key academic and topical vocabulary for the reading and for the unit Writing Task

TEACHING SUGGESTIONS

Encourage students to complete the pre-reading activities in this section in pairs or groups. This will promote a high level of engagement. Once students have completed the activities, check for understanding and offer any clarification.

Encourage or assign your students to keep a vocabulary notebook for new words. This should include new key vocabulary words, parts of speech, definitions (in the students' own words), and contextual sentences. To extend the vocabulary activity in this section, ask students to find synonyms, antonyms, or related terms for the vocabulary items they just practiced. These can then be added to their vocabulary notebooks.

Key vocabulary exercises can also be assigned ahead of time so that you can focus on the reading content and skills in class.

If time permits, have students scan Reading 1 for the key vocabulary just practiced in bold and read the sentences with each term. This will provide additional pre-reading scaffolding.

WHILE READING

PURPOSE

- To introduce, review, and/or practice key academic reading skills
- To practice reading comprehension and annotation skills
- To see and understand key vocabulary in a natural academic context
- To provide information and stimulate ideas on an academic topic
- To help students become more efficient readers

TEACHING SUGGESTIONS

Have students work in pairs or small groups to complete the activities. Students should always be prepared to support their answers from the text, so encourage them to annotate the text as they complete the activities. After students complete the activities, have volunteers share their answers with the class, along with support from the text. If necessary, facilitate clarification by referring back to the text yourself. Use guided questions to help with understanding. For example: *Take a moment to review the final sentences of Paragraph 2. What words discuss a problem?*

READING BETWEEN THE LINES

PURPOSE

- To introduce, expand on, and/or practice key reading skills related to students' ability to infer meaning, text type, purpose, audience, etc.
- To introduce, review, and/or practice key critical thinking skills applied to content from the reading passage

TEACHING SUGGESTIONS

Have students complete the activities in pairs or small groups and share their answers with the class. It is particularly important for students to be able to support their answers using the text at this point. Encourage students to work out any partial or wrong answers by asking a series of clear, guided questions like: *You thought the author meant ... What about this sentence in the reading? What information does it give us? Does this sentence change your mind about your answer?*"

After checking answers, survey students on what they found most challenging in the section. Then have students read the text again for homework, making additional annotations and notes on the challenging skills and content to be shared at the beginning of the next class or in an online forum.

DISCUSSION

PURPOSE

- To give students the opportunity to discuss and offer opinions about what they read
- To think critically about the content of the reading
- To further personalize the topic and issues in Reading 1

TEACHING SUGGESTIONS

Give students three to five minutes to discuss and jot down notes for their answers before discussing them in pairs or small groups. Monitor student groups, taking notes on common mistakes. Then, survey the students on their favorite questions and have groups volunteer to share these answers. You can provide oral or written feedback on common mistakes at the end of the section.

READING 2

Reading 2 is a reading passage on the unit topic from a different angle and often in a different format than Reading 1. It gives students additional exposure to and practice with language and reading skills while helping them generate and refine ideas for their Writing Task. It generally includes rhetorical elements that serve as a structured model for the Writing Task.

PREPARING TO READ

PURPOSE

- To prepare students to understand the content of the reading
- To introduce, review, and/or practice key pre-reading skills
- To introduce and build key academic and topical vocabulary for the reading and for the unit Writing Task

TEACHING SUGGESTIONS

As with Reading 1, encourage students to complete the activities in this section in pairs or small groups to promote a high level of engagement. Circulate among students at this time, taking notes of common areas of difficulty. Once students have completed the activities, check for understanding and offer clarification, paying particular attention to any problem areas you noted.

If you wish to extend the vocabulary activity in this section, elicit other word forms of the key vocabulary. Students can add these word forms to their vocabulary notebooks.

WHILE READING

PURPOSE

- To introduce, review, and/or practice key academic reading skills
- To practice reading comprehension and annotation skills
- To see and understand key vocabulary in a natural academic context
- To provide information and stimulate ideas on an academic topic
- To help students become more efficient readers
- To model aspects or elements of the Writing Task

TEACHING SUGGESTIONS

As with Reading 1, have students work in pairs or small groups to complete the activities. Encourage them to annotate the reading so that they are prepared to support their answers from the text. Elicit answers and explanations from the class. Remember to facilitate clarification by referring back to the text yourself, using clear, guided questions to help with understanding.

Alternatively, separate the class into multiple groups, and assign a paragraph or section of the reading to each groups. (Students should skim the rest of the passage not assigned to them.) Set a time limit for reading. Then do the exercises as a class, with each group responsible for answering and explaining the items that fall within their paragraph or section of the text.

READING BETWEEN THE LINES

PURPOSE

- To introduce, expand on, and/or practice key reading skills related to students' ability to infer meaning, text type, purpose, audience, etc.
- To introduce, review, and/or practice key critical thinking skills applied to content from the reading passage

TEACHING SUGGESTIONS

For Making Inferences activities, have students work in pairs to answer the questions. Instruct pairs to make notes in the margins about the clues from the text they use to answer the questions. Then have pairs meet up with other pairs to compare their clues. Have volunteers share their clues and answers with the class.

For other activity types, such as Recognizing Text Type or Distinguishing Fact and Opinion, have students work in pairs and then share their answers with the class as before. Then promote deeper engagement with guided questions like:

- *How is an essay different from a newspaper article?"*
- *What are common features of a* [text type]?"
- *What words in the sentence tell you that you are reading an opinion and not a fact?*
- *Can you say more about what x means?*

DISCUSSION

PURPOSE

- To personalize and expand on the ideas and content of Reading 2
- To practice synthesizing the content of the unit reading passages

Before students discuss the questions in this section the first time, introduce the key skill of synthesis. Start by defining synthesis (combining and analyzing ideas from multiple sources). Stress its importance in higher education: in college or graduate school, students will be asked to synthesize ideas from a wide range of sources, to think critically about them, to make connections among them, and to add their own ideas. Note: you may need to review this information periodically with your class.

Have students answer the questions in pairs or small groups, and then ask for volunteers to share their answers with the class. Facilitate the discussion, encouraging students to make connections between Reading 1 and Reading 2. If applicable, ask students to relate the content of the unit video to this section. This is also a good context in which to introduce the Writing Task at the beginning of the Critical Thinking section and to have students consider how the content of the reading passages relates to the prompt.

To extend this activity beyond discussion, write the connections students make on the board, and have students take notes. Students can then use their notes to write sentences or a paragraph(s) describing how the ideas in all the sources discussed are connected.

LANGUAGE DEVELOPMENT

Each unit includes the introduction and practice of academic language relevant to the unit topic and readings, and useful for the unit Writing Task. The focus of this section is on vocabulary and/or grammar.

PURPOSE

- To recycle and expand on vocabulary that appears in Reading 1 or Reading 2
- To focus and expand on grammar that appears in Reading 1 or Reading 2
- To expose students to additional corpus-informed, research-based language for the unit topic and level
- To practice language and structures that students can use in the Writing Task

TEACHING SUGGESTIONS

For grammar points, review the Language Box as a class and facilitate answers to any unclear sections. Alternatively, have students review it in pairs and allow time for questions. Then have students work in pairs to complete the accompanying activities. Review students' answers, allowing time for any clarification.

For vocabulary points, have students complete the exercises in pairs. Then, review answers and allow time for any clarification. To extend this activity, have students create sentences using each term and/or make a list of synonyms, antonyms, or related words and phrases for each term. Students should also add relevant language to their vocabulary notebooks. For homework, have students annotate the readings in the unit, underlining or highlighting any language covered in this section.

WRITING

The second half of each unit focuses on the productive skill of writing. It begins with the prompt for the Writing Task and systematically equips students with the grammar and skills to plan for, prepare, and execute the task successfully.

CRITICAL THINKING

PURPOSE

- To introduce the Writing Task.
- To notice and analyze features of Reading 2 related to the Writing Task.
- To help generate, develop, and organize ideas for the Writing Task.
- To teach and practice the lower-order critical thinking skills of remembering, understanding, and applying knowledge through practical brainstorming and organizational activities

- To teach and practice the higher-order critical thinking skills of analyzing, evaluating, and creating in order to prepare students for success in the Writing Task and, more generally, in the college classroom

TEACHING SUGGESTIONS

Encourage students to work through this section collaboratively in pairs or small groups to promote a high level of engagement. Facilitate their learning and progress by circulating and checking in on students as they work through this section. If time permits, have groups exchange and evaluate one another's work.

Note: Students will often be directed back to this section to review, revise, and expand on their initial ideas and notes for the Writing Task.

GRAMMAR FOR WRITING

PURPOSE

- To introduce and practice grammar that is relevant to the Writing Task
- To introduce and practice grammar that often presents trouble for students at this level of academic writing

TEACHING SUGGESTIONS

Review any skills boxes in this section as a class, allowing time to answer questions and clarify points of confusion. Then have students work on the activities in pairs or small groups, before eliciting answers as a class.

ACADEMIC WRITING SKILLS

PURPOSE

- To present and practice academic writing skills needed to be successful in college or graduate school
- To focus on specific language and skills relevant to the Writing Task

TEACHING SUGGESTIONS

Have students read any skills boxes on their own. Check understanding by asking guided questions like:

- *What do you notice about the parallel structure examples?*
- *What are some other examples of parallel structure?*
- *How would you describe parallel structure based on the information and examples you just read?*

Provide clarification as necessary, offering and eliciting more examples. Have students find examples in the unit readings if possible.

Students can work in pairs to complete the exercises and then share their answers with the class. Alternatively, assign exercises for homework.

WRITING TASK

PURPOSE

- To work collaboratively in preparation for the Writing Task
- To revisit, revise, and expand on work done in the Critical Thinking section
- To provide an opportunity for students to synthesize the language, skills, and ideas presented and generated in the unit
- To help students plan, draft, revise, and edit their writing

TEACHING SUGGESTIONS

Depending on time and class level, students can complete the preparation activities for homework or in class. If conducted in class, have students work on their own to complete the Plan section. They can then share their plans in pairs. Give students time to revise their plans based on feedback from their partners.

Depending on time, students can write their first drafts at home or in class. Encourage students to refer to the Task Checklist before and after writing their first drafts. The checklist can also be used in a peer review of first drafts in class.

Note: At this stage, encourage students to focus on generating and organizing their ideas, and answering the prompt, rather than perfecting their grammar, which they will focus on during the Edit stage using the Language Checklist.

Even with a peer review, it is important to provide written feedback for your students, either on their first or second drafts. When doing so, look for common mistakes in student writing. Select at least one problem sentence or area from each student's draft, and conduct an edit correction exercise either as a class or in an online discussion forum. You can also select and review a well-written sentence from each draft to serve as models and to provide positive reinforcement.

ON CAMPUS

Each unit concludes with a unique spread that teaches students concepts and skills that go beyond traditional reading and writing academic skills.

PURPOSE
- To familiarize students with all aspects of the North American college experience
- To enable students to interact and participate successfully in the college classroom
- To prepare students to navigate typical North American college campus life

TEACHING SUGGESTIONS
PREPARING TO READ
Begin with an open discussion by asking students what they know about the topic. For example:
- *What is a study plan?*
- *Have you ever written an email to a teacher or professor?*
- *How do college students choose a major?*
- *What is a virtual classroom?*

You can also write the question on the board and assign as pair work, and have students share their answers with the class.

WHILE READING
Have students read the text and complete the accompanying activities. Have them read again and check their work. You can extend these activities by asking the following questions:
- *What did you find most interesting in this reading passage?*
- *What did you understand more clearly during the second reading?*
- *Who do you think wrote the text? Why?*

PRACTICE
Have students read any skills boxes silently. Give them two minutes to discuss the information with partners before they complete the exercises. Elicit from some volunteers how the exercises practice what they read in the text.

REAL-WORLD APPLICATION
Depending on time, you may want to assign the activities in this section as homework. Having students collaborate on these real-world tasks either inside or outside of the classroom simulates a common practice in college and graduate school. At the beginning of the week you can set up a schedule so that several student groups present their work during class throughout the week.

To extend this section, assign small related research projects, as applicable. For example, have students research and report on three websites with information on choosing a college major.

PRISM WRITING TASK RUBRIC

CATEGORY	CRITERIA	SCORE
Content and Development	• Writing completes the task and fully answers the prompt. • Content is meaningful and interesting. • Main points and ideas are fully developed with good support and logic.	

Organization	• Writing is well-organized and follows the conventions of academic writing:
	  • Paragraph – topic sentence, supporting details, concluding sentence
	  • Essay – introduction with thesis, body paragraphs, conclusion
	• Rhetorical mode(s) used is appropriate to the writing task.	

Coherence, Clarity, and Unity	• Sentences within a paragraph flow logically with appropriate transitions; paragraphs within an essay flow logically with appropriate transitions. • Sentences and ideas are clear and make sense to the reader. • All sentences in a paragraph relate to the topic sentence; all paragraphs in an essay relate to the thesis.	
Vocabulary	• Vocabulary, including expressions and transition language, is accurate, appropriate, and varied. • Writing shows mastery of unit key vocabulary and Language Development.	
Grammar and Writing Skills	• Grammar is accurate, appropriate, and varied. • Writing shows mastery of unit Grammar for Writing and Language Development. • Sentence types are varied and used appropriately. • Level of formality shows an understanding of audience and purpose. • Mechanics (capitalization, punctuation, indentation, and spelling) are strong. • Writing shows mastery of unit Academic Writing Skills.	

How well does the response meet the criteria?	Recommended Score
At least 90%	20
At least 75%	15
At least 60%	10
At least 50%	5
Less than 50%	0
Total Score Possible per Section	20
Total Score Possible	100

Feedback:

STUDENT'S BOOK ANSWER KEY

UNIT 1
ACTIVATE YOUR KNOWLEDGE
page 15

1 *Possible answers*: Many people think it is better to see animals in the wild because they can then be appreciated in their natural habitat. However, seeing animals in a zoo means that people who cannot travel can still see animals from other parts of the world.

2 *Answers will vary.*

3 *Possible answers*: People keep animals in their homes for companionship. Some research has suggested that stroking a cat can reduce stress, dogs can help owners feel more secure when walking or living alone, and pets can help children develop a sense of responsibility.

4 *Possible answers*: Many regions rely on animals for heavy work, such as pulling ploughs or transporting goods or people. Animals can provide materials such as wool, suede, and leather. Animals also provide meat and dairy produce, such as milk and cheese.

5 *Answers will vary.*

WATCH AND LISTEN

Exercise 1 page 16
Answers will vary.

Exercise 2 page 16
Possible answers:
1 To get food
2 They help/protect each other.
3 They both eat fish so live in similar places.

Exercise 3 page 17
a 4   b 1   c 5   d 2   e 3

Exercise 4 page 17
1 T
2 F; The dolphins push the <u>fish</u> ~~egrets~~ onto the shore.
3 F; When the fish are <u>out of</u> ~~in~~ the water, the dolphins start eating.
4 F; The dolphins always use their <u>right</u> ~~left~~ sides to push the fish.
5 DNS

Exercise 5 page 17
Answers will vary.

READING 1

Exercise 1 page 18
1 endangered   2 species   3 chemicals   4 pollute
5 destroys   6 due to   7 natural   8 protect

Exercise 2 page 18
Possible answers:

endangered animals	extinct animals
giant panda	Tyrannosaurus rex
Chinese alligator	woolly mammoth
Indian elephant	dodo
white rhinoceros	Caspian tiger
sea turtle	sabre tooth tiger
	woolly rhinoceros

Exercise 3 page 19
Added to endangered species column: Arabian oryx, seals, tigers, crocodiles, whales, tuna, sharks

Exercise 4 page 20
a 3   b 1   c 4   d 2

Exercise 5 page 20
1 Humans
2 Their habitats are destroyed.
3 For food, for fur to make coats, and skin to make bags and shoes, for sport, to make medicines and teas from their bones.
4 Whales, tuna and sharks
5 We can try not to pollute natural areas and refuse to buy products made from animals' body parts.
6 Governments can make it against the law to hunt, fish, or trade in endangered species.
7 They can provide funding for animal sanctuaries and zoos where endangered animals can be bred and then released back into the wild.

Exercise 6 page 20
1 face a financial penalty
2 refusing to buy
3 against the law
4 provide funding for
5 cooperate by taking these steps

Exercise 7 page 21
1 *Possible answers*: perfume, fur coats, leather gloves, plastic bags, some glues, and fabric softeners
2–3 *Answers will vary.*

READING 2

Exercise 1 page 21
1 common   2 fatal   3 disease   4 cruel   5 major
6 survive   7 native

Exercise 2 page 21
1 squirrels
2–3 *Answers will vary.*

Exercise 3 page 22
1 An invasive species is a plant or animal that arrives in an area where it is not native.
2 Gray squirrels were introduced from North America by people who wanted them as a fashionable addition to their homes.
3 Red and gray squirrels both have long tails, large eyes, small ears, and powerful back legs.
4 Red squirrels are smaller and weaker than gray squirrels. The parapox virus is fatal to red squirrels and they are affected by the loss of their natural woodland habitat.
5 Gray squirrels are larger and stronger, they are more intelligent and adaptable, they can use food provided by humans, and they are immune to the parapox virus.

Exercise 4 page 22
1 gray   2 fewer   3 fatter   4 able   5 kills   6 pest
7 few   8 aren't

Exercise 5 page 22
Possible answers:
1 Ships; wood products; garden plants, the pet trade, illegal trading
2 Because they damage trees, they eat humans' waste food and they carry a virus that kills red squirrels
3 Perhaps for nostalgic reasons, because they see them as traditionally "British"
4 Because it is an island, and the sea acts as a natural defense against alien species

Exercise 6 page 24
1 *Possible answers*: habitat destruction, disease, climate
2–4 *Answers will vary.*

LANGUAGE DEVELOPMENT

Exercise 1 page 24
a cooperate   b affect   c release   d survive
e contrast   f attach

Exercise 2 page 25
1 weaker than   2 healthier than
3 more successful than   4 more endangered than

CRITICAL THINKING

Exercise 1 page 26
Possible answers:

red squirrels	both	gray squirrels
red in color only 140,000 left not seen as pests smaller and lighter shorter tail store less fat so more likely to die in winter live high up in trees less intelligent can't survive in an urban environment can't eat human food can die from the parapox virus	live in Great Britain have a long tail large eyes small ears powerful back legs can carry the parapox virus	gray in color very common seen as pests larger and heavier longer tail store more fat so survive winter more easily spend most of their time on the ground more intelligent can survive in an urban environment can eat human food can't die from the parapox virus

Exercise 2 page 26
Possible answers:
1 The whale shark is larger than the tiger shark.
2 Both sharks have a gray color on their backs and sides and a lighter underside.
3 The tiger shark has stripes on its back and the whale shark has dots.
4 The whale shark has a larger mouth, but the tiger shark has many teeth.
5 The whale shark has a longer tail and wider fins, but the fin on the back of a tiger shark is larger in relation to its body size.

Exercise 3 page 27
1 the tiger shark
2 the whale shark
3 the tiger shark
4 the whale shark
5 the whale shark
6 the tiger shark

Exercise 4 page 28
Possible answers:

whale shark	both	tiger shark
gray-blue in color with white belly and white spots	chondrichthyes (fish) lives in the ocean	gray-brown in color with white belly and white stripes
has no teeth		has teeth
longer (18–32 feet)		shorter (10–14 feet)
longer tail and wider fins		shorter tail and fins but its fin is bigger in comparison to its body size
heavier (40,000 pounds)		lighter (1900 pounds)
eats plankton, krill and other small animals		eats tuna, dolphins and turtles
currently endangered		not at risk of extinction
no recorded attacks on humans		111 attacks on humans

GRAMMAR FOR WRITING

Exercise 1 page 29

subject	verb		prepositional phrase	
1 The tiger shark	lives		in tropical oceans.	

linker	subject	verb	adjective	
2 However,	the whale shark	isn't	dangerous.	

subject	verb	object	prepositional phrase	
3 The tiger shark	has	markings	on its skin.	

subject	verb	object	verb	object
4 The whale shark	has	a large mouth and	eats	plankton.

Exercise 2 page 29
1 The whale shark is gray-blue and has light spots on its body.
2 The tiger shark is gray-brown and has a stripe pattern on its body.
3 The tiger shark eats large sea creatures and can be dangerous to humans.
4 The whale shark is not aggressive or dangerous to swim with.
5 The tiger shark is not an endangered or protected species.
6 The whale shark is an endangered and protected species.

Exercise 3 page 30
Possible answers:
1 The whale shark is gray-blue and has light spots on its body, whereas the tiger shark is gray-brown and has a stripe pattern on its body.
2 The tiger shark eats large sea creatures and can be dangerous to humans, whereas the whale shark is not aggressive or dangerous to swim with.
3 The tiger shark is not an endangered or protected species, whereas the whale shark is an endangered and protected species.

Exercise 4 page 30
Possible answers:
1 Both the red (squirrel) and the gray squirrel have long tails. / Both red (squirrels) and gray squirrels have long tails.
2 Neither the red (squirrel) nor the gray squirrel live on the Isle of Man. / Neither red (squirrels) nor gray squirrels live on the Isle of Man.
3 Neither red (squirrels) nor gray squirrels are meat-eaters.
4 Neither the gray nor the red squirrel is an endangered species.
5 Both red (squirrels) and gray squirrels live in forests.

ACADEMIC WRITING SKILLS

Exercise 1 page 31
1 c, d
2 a
3 Each paragraph has 1–6 supporting sentences, and they differ in length. This tells me that there is no "correct" number of sentences in a paragraph.

Exercise 2 page 32
b, c

WRITING TASK

Exercise 1 page 32
Answers will vary.

Exercise 2 page 32
Answers will vary.

Exercise 3 page 33
Answers will vary.

Exercise 4 page 33
Answers will vary.

Exercise 5 page 33
Answers will vary.

Exercise 6 page 33
Answers will vary.

ON CAMPUS

Exercise 1 page 34
Answers will vary.

Exercise 2 page 35
1 a, e
2 d, f
3 b, c

Exercise 3 page 35
1 F; If a student plagiarizes then it's dishonest and it has to be reported to the Dean of students.
2 F; Students should cite sources of photos and graphs.
3 T
4 T
5 T
6 F; If students are having trouble they should see their professor.

Exercise 4 page 35
Answers will vary.

Exercise 5 page 35
Answers will vary.

Exercise 6 page 35
Answers will vary.

Exercise 7 page 35
Answers will vary.

Exercise 8 page 35
Answers will vary.

UNIT 2
ACTIVATE YOUR KNOWLEDGE
page 37
Answers will vary.

WATCH AND LISTEN

Exercise 1 page 38
1 *Possible answers*: Aurora, Grand Canyon, Great Barrier Reef, Harbor of Rio de Janeiro, Mount Everest, Paricutin, Victoria Falls
2–3 *Answers will vary.*

Exercise 2 page 38
Possible answers:
1 The U.S.
2 Millions of years old
3 The U.S. government

Exercise 3 page 39
a 4 b 2 c 1 d 5 e 3 f 6

Exercise 4 page 39
1 b
2 b
3 c
4 b
5 a

Exercise 5 page 39
Answers will vary.

READING 1

Exercise 1 page 40
a greenhouse gas b cause c atmosphere d climate
e global warming f threaten g ecosystem
h fossil fuels

Exercise 2 page 40
1 It has melted.
2 global warming
3 The Arctic, the Alps, Alaska, and other mountain areas around the world
4 Sea levels will rise, and many coastal areas will be underwater.

Exercise 3 page 42
solution to the problem 4
changing ecosystems 2
melting glaciers 1
causes of climate change 3

Exercise 4 page 42
1 global temperatures
2 extinction
3 Global sea levels
4 mangrove forests

5 coral reefs
6 farming
7 CO_2 levels

Exercise 5 page 43
1 Argentina
2 Northwest Passage
3 to provide land for growing food
4 asthma
5 methane, carbon dioxide
6 burning fossil fuels and cutting down trees
7 stop burning fossil fuels, start using renewable energy

Exercise 6 page 43
c

Exercise 7 page 43
Possible answers:
1 an increase in land for farming, new transportation routes, increased fresh water, melt water can be used for hydroelectric power
2 the implementation can be expensive, some people say that things like solar panels and wind turbines are ugly, some renewable energies aren't suitable for every country
3 it's too expensive, it's a global problem so one country may not be able to make a change, big businesses can make a bigger impact on global warming than governments

READING 2

Exercise 1 page 44
Possible answers:
1 They put oxygen into the atmosphere, provide shade, and are home to many species of animals.
2 to clear land for farming or to provide wood for building
3 The earth's temperature will rise, erosion will cause dust storms and floods, animals will lose their habitats.

Exercise 2 page 44
1 absorb   2 Farming   3 Logging   4 rainforest
5 construction   6 effects   7 destruction

Exercise 3 page 46
1 deforestation
2 effects
3 animals
4 crops
5 decade
6 erosion
7 warming
8 habitats
9 protected
10 environment

Exercise 4 page 46
1 ~~olive~~ palm
2 ~~ten years~~ two or three years
3 ~~U.S.~~ Texas
4 ~~protects~~ destroys
5 ~~oxygen~~ carbon dioxide
6 ~~Small-scale~~ Large-scale

Exercise 5 page 46
Possible answers:
1 logging and farming that are done on a large scale by giant corporations
2 The earth's climate will become much warmer, and thousands of plants and animals will become extinct.
3 Many of the foods we eat and medicines we use come from forests, e.g., mushrooms come from forests and some medicines are made from tree bark.

Exercise 6 page 47
Possible answers:
1 Low-lying islands, cities near coastlines, and places with more rain and storms will have too much water. Places that are normally dry, such as many African countries, will become even drier.
2 As the ice caps and forests disappear, the animals that live there have no place to live and they die out.

LANGUAGE DEVELOPMENT

Exercise 1 page 47
1 issue
2 predict
3 consequences
4 trend
5 areas
6 annual
7 challenge
8 contributes to

Exercise 2 page 48
1 c   2 a   3 e   4 g   5 b   6 f   7 d

Exercise 3 page 48
1 power plant
2 greenhouse gases
3 climate change
4 carbon dioxide
5 environmental groups
6 natural resource
7 tropical rainforests

CRITICAL THINKING

Exercise 1 page 49

CAUSE	EFFECT
commercial farming by big business	climate change
industrial logging	damage to animal habitats
farming by local people	

Exercise 2 page 50
(starting from any point in the circle but in the following order)
1 CO_2 enters atmosphere and traps heat (greenhouse effect)
2 global warming
3 less rain
4 forests dry out
5 fires
6 more CO_2 emissions

Exercise 3 page 50
Possible answers:

CAUSE	EFFECT
greenhouse gases	melting glaciers
growing world population	rising sea levels
burning fossil fuels	some cities and islands will be underwater
cutting down trees	habitat loss
commercial farming	species extinction
industrial logging	health problems, e.g. asthma
clear cutting by local farmers	
destruction of rain forests	

Exercise 4 page 50
Answers will vary.

GRAMMAR FOR WRITING

Exercise 1 page 51
2 causes / results in
3 caused by / due to / the result of
4 caused by / due to / the result of

Exercise 2 page 51
1 results
2 due
3 causes
4 caused
5 result
6 result

Exercise 3 page 52
1 because of
2 because
3 because of
4 because

ACADEMIC WRITING SKILLS

Exercise 1 page 52
Main idea: Plastic water bottles hurt both the consumer and the environment.
Cross out: In the 1970s, the United States was the world's biggest exporter of fossil fuels.

Exercise 2 page 53
1 Supporting sentences:
   Plastic bottles contain two harmful chemicals, BPA and phthalates.
   Plastic bottles are extremely harmful to the environment.
2 Both chemicals cause health problems for adults and children. This is a fact.
3 Fact: Most plastic bottles are not recycled.
   Fact: Transporting bottles requires an enormous amount of fossil fuels.
   Fact: Plastic bottles take many decades to break down.

WRITING TASK

Exercise 1 page 54
Answers will vary.

Exercise 2 page 54
Answers will vary.

Exercise 3 page 54
Answers will vary.

Exercise 4 page 54
Answers will vary.

Exercise 5 page 54
Answers will vary.

Exercise 6 page 55
Answers will vary.

Exercise 7 page 55
Answers will vary.

Exercise 8 page 55
Answers will vary.

Exercise 9 page 55
Answers will vary.

ON CAMPUS

Exercise 1 page 56
Answers will vary.

Exercise 2 page 57
1 advisor
2 required courses
3 prerequisites
4 electives

Exercise 3 page 57
1 F; Management 200 is a required course for business majors only.
2 T
3 F; Sociology 115 is an elective course for business majors.
4 T
5 T
6 F; The courses have different numbers of credits – from two to four.

Exercise 4 page 57
Answers will vary.

Exercise 5 page 57
Answers will vary.

Exercise 6 page 57
Answers will vary.

UNIT 3
ACTIVATE YOUR KNOWLEDGE
page 59
1 *Possible answers*: car, bike, motorcycle, bus, rickshaw, truck
2 *Answers will vary.*

WATCH AND LISTEN

Exercise 1 page 60
Answers will vary.

Exercise 2 page 60
Answers will vary.

Exercise 3 page 61
1 flew
2 helped
3 worked
4 had
5 changed

Exercise 4 page 61
1 b
2 c
3 c
4 a
5 a

Exercise 5 page 61
Answers will vary.

Exercise 6 page 61
Answers will vary.

READING 1

Exercise 1 page 62
1 The problem is traffic congestion.
2 The vehicle in the second photograph is a kind of electric car. It could be a solution because it would cause less pollution and be quieter than cars are now. It was taken in Masdar City in Abu Dhabi.
3 The city in photo 1 has a lot of traffic and pollution whereas the city in photo 2 has clean transportation and no congestion.

Exercise 2 page 63
1 public transportation   2 outskirts   3 rail
4 Traffic congestion   5 destination   6 commuter
7 connect

Exercise 3 page 63
1 a wall around the city and narrow streets
2 Personal Rapid Transit. It consists of small electric vehicles that run on solar energy. They are pulled by magnets along a fixed route.
3 an underground rail system and a light rail transit system
4 The planners decided not to finish building the PRT system.

Exercise 4 page 65
1 traffic congestion
2 45 minutes
3 solar power
4 not allowed
5 24 billion
6 2025; 50,000

Exercise 5 page 65
Possible answers:
1 An expanding economy means more people have more money for health, education, travel, and life in general. A rising population means there are more people to work and help build the economy.
2 It will be near the airport, so there may be noise and air pollution. It might not have good schools, shopping, or entertainment.
3 It was too expensive, and there were other, cheaper transportation solutions.

Exercise 6 page 65
Answers will vary.

READING 2

Exercise 1 page 66

1 cycle   2 emergency   3 engineering   4 fuel
5 government   6 vehicles   7 practical

Exercise 2 page 66

1 ferry, bus, subway/underground
2 *Answers will vary.*

Exercise 3 page 68

b

Exercise 4 page 68

stress, economic losses, emergency services cannot get through traffic, and negative effects on the environment

Exercise 5 page 68

1 tunnels
2 travel
3 result
4 fuel
5 jobs
6 health
7 traffic
8 bus
9 congestion / traffic
10 night

Exercise 6 page 68

Possible answers:

1 high blood pressure, insomnia, trouble concentrating
2 People might not re-elect the politicians that approved the tax.
3 The bus stop might not be close to their home or work. They might have to wait a long time for the bus to arrive.

Exercise 7 page 69

1 *Possible answers:* Yes, lots of cities have problems with long commute times, traffic congestion, pollution, etc.
2 *Possible answers:* The solutions probably wouldn't work in other big cities because big cities are already built, whereas Masdar is a new city.
3 *Answers will vary.*

LANGUAGE DEVELOPMENT

Exercise 1 page 69

1 c   2 a   3 d   4 g   5 e   6 f   7 b

Exercise 2 page 69

1 Traffic congestion
2 public transportation
3 bike lane
4 parking restrictions
5 Rush hour
6 carpool
7 road rage

Exercise 3 page 70

1 ~~need~~ require
2 ~~try~~ attempt
3 ~~make~~ produce
4 ~~lower~~ reduce
5 ~~use in an inefficient way~~ waste
6 ~~think~~ consider
7 ~~stop~~ prevent
8 ~~get~~ convince

CRITICAL THINKING

Exercise 1 page 71

Possible answers:

problem	goal
traffic congestion causing wasted time, stress, road rage, economic losses, problems for emergency services and the environment	to reduce traffic congestion and its effects

solutions	advantages/disadvantages
engineering – building new road with wider lanes and tunnels	**+** people can travel at the same time tunnels and bridges direct drivers away from congested areas
	– extremely high cost more roads may result in more traffic
tax on fuel or travel on a freeway	**+** people think more carefully about using their cars
	– some people cannot afford to drive their cars and they may have to give up their jobs it may be unpopular with voters
promote cycling	**+** health benefits does not pollute the air
	– not practical in every climate dangerous in heavy traffic
persuade people to use buses	**+** allows flexibility for drivers but reduces congestion in the center of the city
	– there are no buses at night for people who work late shifts

decision	reason
encourage alternative forms of transportation e.g. cycling, buses	it reduces the amount of traffic on the roads and has a positive effect on the environment

Exercise 2 page 72
Possible answers:
2 Although there is a bus service joining the residential and economic areas, this may increase the congestion on the main route into and out of the city center as the buses have to make frequent stops.
3 The fact that the majority of people start and finish work at the same time means that there is a lot of congestion as everyone is going into the city or going home at the same time.
4 There is a junction with traffic lights at one end of the bridge, which may also cause/add to the congestion problems.

Exercise 3 page 73
Possible answers:

Problem	Goal(s)
There is only a single two lane motorway joining the residential area to the area of schools and offices.	To stop traffic congestion in the city.

Exercise 4 page 73
Possible answers:

build a tunnel	+ People would be happy as they could still drive
	− Expensive to build, will take a long time, would eventually fill with traffic
encourage people to cycle	+ It would be cheap and quick
	− It would be too hot to cycle over a desert, it can be dangerous, not many people would want to change to cycling
park-and-ride bus system	+ Fairly quick, people would like it more than cycling
	− Designed to keep people from driving in the center, but the problem is getting to the center, people don't like buses, it would be quite expensive, the bus will get stuck in congestion

move the residential area to the other side of the river	+ Long-term solution that completely solves the congestion problem
	− Very, very expensive, people won't want to move
road tax	+ Cheap and quick to implement, money for the government
	− It may not stop people from using their cars—they'll just pay since they don't have a better option
ferry	+ people could drive their cars on to the ferry, which would reduce road traffic, requires less building than a new bridge/road
	− there will be a queue for cars to board, not very frequent, may be expensive to run, fairly expensive to build, it would take a while to build a port

Exercise 5 page 73
Answers will vary.

GRAMMAR FOR WRITING

Exercise 1 page 74
1 If we move the offices and schools next to the houses, we will have fewer traffic problems. / We will have fewer traffic problems if we move the offices and schools next to the houses.
2 If we have a ferry over the river, fewer people will use the bridge. / Fewer people will use the bridge if we have a ferry over the river.
3 Fewer cars will use the roads if we increase the price of fuel. / If we increase the price of fuel, fewer cars will use the roads.
4 If we change the office hours, cars won't all use the road at the same time. / Cars will not all use the road at the same time if we change the office hours.
5 If we build a railway line, people will be able to use the train instead of their cars. / People will be able to use the train instead of their cars if we build a railway line.

Exercise 2 page 74

Possible answers:

2 Pollution won't be reduced if we don't use cleaner transportation. / Pollution won't be reduced unless we use cleaner transportation.

3 If we don't provide a solution, people won't get to work on time. / Unless we provide a solution, people won't get to work on time.

4 We won't solve the traffic problem if we don't build houses closer to the business areas. / We won't solve the traffic problem unless we build houses closer to the business area.

5 If the city doesn't invest in a PRT, there won't be less congestion. / Unless the city invests in a PRT, there won't be less congestion.

ACADEMIC WRITING SKILLS

Exercise 1 page 75

Paragraph 1: b

Paragraph 2: a

WRITING TASK

Exercise 1 page 76

Answers will vary.

Exercise 2 page 76

Answers will vary.

Exercise 3 page 76

Answers will vary.

Exercise 4 page 77

Answers will vary.

Exercise 5 page 77

Answers will vary.

Exercise 6 page 77

Answers will vary.

Exercise 7 page 77

Answers will vary.

ON CAMPUS

Exercise 1 page 78

Answers will vary.

Exercise 2 page 79

1 a   2 b   3 b   4 a

Exercise 3 page 79

1 The main idea of the map is Masdar City.

2 There are three related ideas: energy use, traffic congestion and problems.

3 There are three ideas about energy use: renewable energy, city walls and narrow streets.

4 The sun symbol is used to represent the use of solar energy.

Exercise 4 page 79

Answers will vary.

Exercise 5 page 79

Answers will vary.

Exercise 6 page 79

Answers will vary.

UNIT 4
ACTIVATE YOUR KNOWLEDGE

page 81

1 The celebration shown is a wedding.

2–3 *Answers will vary.*

WATCH AND LISTEN

Exercise 1 page 82

Answers will vary.

Exercise 2 page 82

Possible answers:

1 People dress up in costumes and masks and go from door to door asking for candy.

2 The number of pumpkins

3 Costumes

Exercise 3 page 83

1 candy

2 costumes

3 tradition

4 good

5 person

Exercise 4 page 83

1 F; Tens of millions ~~billions~~ of trick-or-treaters celebrate Halloween.

2 F; The most popular ~~expensive~~ variety of candy is chocolate.

3 F; Illinois produces a lot of pumpkins ~~costumes~~.

4 T

5 DNS

Exercise 5 page 83

Possible answers:

1 I think it's more popular with children because they would like to dress in costumes and eat candy.

2 Because they want to look frightening. / Because it's fun.

3 In the United States people spend the most money on Christmas. They spend money on presents, food and drink and decorations.

Exercise 6 page 83

Answers will vary.

READING 1

Exercise 1 page 84

1 cultures 2 exchange 3 expect 4 greet
5 formal 6 appearance 7 relationship

Exercise 2 page 85
Answers will vary.

Exercise 3 page 85
Answers will vary.

Exercise 4 page 85
Answers will vary.

Exercise 5 page 85
e

Exercise 6 page 87

custom/ behavior	Brazil	Japan	India
greeting	1 kiss 2 shake hands with	3 shake hands 4 bowing	5 oldest 6 women 7 men
gifts	8 home	9 refuse 10 token	11 necessary 12 white flowers
business behavior	13 gift	14 both hands 15 read it	16 First 17 no 18 Appointments
dress/ appearance	19 well	20 formally	21 formal
punctuality	22 30 minutes late	23 early	24 on time

Exercise 7 page 87
Possible answers:

1 They might think you are trying to bribe them or "buy" a favor.
2 Brazilians are accustomed to touching, so they might be offended if you move away.
3 Hierarchy is important in Japanese culture.
4 They want to maintain a harmonious relationship.
5 People become offended and relationships could suffer or possibly end.

Exercise 8 page 88
Answers will vary.

READING 2

Exercise 1 page 88

1 ceremony 2 couple 3 beliefs 4 engaged
5 theme 6 reception 7 relatives

Exercise 2 page 90

1 The people in the photos are getting married. They are under water, on a beach and dressed as characters from a movie.
2–3 *Answers will vary.*

Exercise 3 page 90
Answers will vary.

Exercise 4 page 90
theme weddings 4
adventure weddings 2
reasons for the popularity of non-traditional weddings 5
destination weddings 3
choices for the couple who want a nontraditional wedding 1

Exercise 5 page 90
a

Exercise 6 page 90

1 ~~suit~~ dress
2 ~~Frank~~ Cathy
3 ~~close to~~ far from
4 ~~theme~~ adventure
5 ~~adventure~~ theme
6 ~~few~~ many

Exercise 7 page 91

1 *Possible answers*: Most American couples choose to have traditional weddings because it's what their family and friends expect them to do.
2 *Possible answers*: <u>Adventure</u>: Some guests might not be able to participate if the activity is difficult or dangerous. It could also be expensive.
<u>Theme</u>: Some traditional family members might disapprove. It could be expensive.
3 *Answers will vary.*

Exercise 8 page 91
Answers will vary.

LANGUAGE DEVELOPMENT

Exercise 1 page 92

1 We tend to tip the waiter in a restaurant.
2 Formal weddings tend to be less common these days.
3 Anniversaries can be important.
4 Common hand gestures like waving can be misunderstood in a different culture.
5 In Mexico, most old people live with their children.

Exercise 2 page 93

1 In the past, the bride's family usually paid for the wedding.
2 Outdoor weddings are often cheaper than church weddings.

3 Professionals sometimes get upset if you don't use their correct title.
4 Cultural knowledge is frequently helpful in business situations.
5 In Japan, you should always arrive on time for an appointment.

Exercise 3 page 93
1 brief
2 serious
3 separate
4 certain
5 important
6 obvious
7 common

CRITICAL THINKING

Exercise 1 page 94
Possible answers:

	text
paragraph 1 main idea	Many couples are choosing nontraditional weddings these days
paragraph 2	*Topic: adventure wedding* *Example: Couple got married underwater* *Advantage: Combine their love of scuba diving with their love for each other*
paragraph 3	Topic: destination wedding Example: couple got married in Scotland Disadvantage: cost
paragraph 4	Topic: theme wedding Example: Harry Potter theme Advantage: fun
conclusion	Wedding styles change, but their purpose—to celebrate a marriage—will never change.

Exercise 2 page 95
Answers will vary.

GRAMMAR FOR WRITING

Exercise 1 page 96
1 c   2 a   3 b

Exercise 2 page 96
Possible answers:
1 Most couples in the United States still prefer an old-fashioned wedding, but increasingly, couples are considering one-of-a-kind options based on the things they enjoy doing and believe.

2 Frank's idea for their wedding was very different from Cathy's dream of a big, old-fashioned ceremony in a church.
3 According to Serena Lessler, unusual wedding themes include country music, superheroes, fairy tales, Victorian England, a Hawaiian luau, and others.

ACADEMIC WRITING SKILLS

Exercise 1 page 97
Possible answers:
1 In the article "Customs around the world," author Andy Schmidt says it is important for tourists to learn about the customs of other countries in order to prevent cultural misunderstandings in the places they are visiting.
2 indirect speech, synonyms, change the order of words or phrases
3 important details about each of the three countries in the article
4 Brazil: touching, punctuality; Japan: touching, business cards, dress, gifts, punctuality; India: formality, punctuality, the Indian custom of not saying no. This gives a few details from each country so is about the right amount of information.
5 Four references: Andy Schmidt says … , Schmidt focuses on … , According to the author, … The author stresses …
6 It's the topic sentence of the second paragraph: "I definitely agree with the author's main point."
7 examples from her own experience
8 She restates the main idea. "In short, …"

WRITING TASK

Exercise 1 page 98
Answers will vary.

Exercise 2 page 99
Answers will vary.

Exercise 3 page 99
Answers will vary.

Exercise 4 page 99
Answers will vary.

Exercise 5 page 99
Answers will vary.

Exercise 6 page 99
Answers will vary.

Exercise 7 page 99
Answers will vary.

ON CAMPUS

Exercise 1 page 100
Answers will vary.

Exercise 2 page 101
1 Dr. Alcott wants to see Linda because she has sent a rude, informal email that doesn't apologize for missing her classes.
2 Dr. Alcott's tone is very serious and formal. Linda's tone is friendly and informal.
3 a, b, c, e, f, g, h

Exercise 3 page 101
(correct spelling and punctuation throughout)
LinSun123@abc.edu (school email)
To: David Alcott
Re: Missed classes in History 104 (informative subject line)
Dear Professor Alcott, (formal tone and professor's formal name)
I am in your 10:00 section of History 104. I want to apologize for missing several classes in the last two weeks. (apologizes) I had a problem with my work schedule. I have tried to make up the work that I missed. (offers to make up for her mistake) I did all of the reading and borrowed notes from a classmate, but I still have a few questions about the material. Could I come to your office hours tomorrow to discuss them with you?
Sincerely, (signed her message)
Linda Sun

Exercise 4 page 101
Answers will vary.

Exercise 5 page 101
Answers will vary.

Exercise 6 page 101
Answers will vary.

UNIT 5
ACTIVATE YOUR KNOWLEDGE
page 103
1 *Answers will vary.*
2 *Possible answers*: Healthy people eat a balanced diet, exercise regularly, get enough sleep, have a good mental attitude
3 *Possible answers*: They avoid overeating or eating the wrong things. They avoid smoking, drugs, and alcohol.
4 *Possible answers*: walking, jogging, swimming, biking, yoga, tennis, and all kinds of team sports

WATCH AND LISTEN

Exercise 1 page 104
Answers will vary.

Exercise 2 page 104
Answers will vary.

Exercise 3 page 105
1 d
2 e
3 a
4 b
5 c

Exercise 4 page 105
Possible answers:
1 Two decades ago
2 They will be more realistic/larger.
3 Some beverage companies have already made changes.
4 $2 billion
5 What's in the food we're feeding our families

Exercise 5 page 105
Possible answers:
1 Because people might not buy their food/drinks
2 Because they want people to eat/drink more
3 Michelle Obama would probably support healthier public school lunches and higher taxes on beverages.

Exercise 6 page 105
Answers will vary.

READING 1

Exercise 1 page 106
a active b reduce c serious d self-esteem
e calories f recognize g moderate

Exercise 2 page 106
a basketball
b racquetball
c housework/cleaning
d soccer
e gardening
f jogging/running
g swimming
h cycling

Exercise 3 page 108
c

Exercise 4 page 108
a 3 b 1 c 5 d X e 2 f 4

Exercise 5 page 108
1 heart disease, type 2 diabetes, stroke, some cancers
2 mood, self-esteem, sleep quality
3 7+ hours
4 the cost of a field or court
5 at off-peak times
6 running shoes
7 a park

Exercise 6 page 109

Possible answers:

1 It helps improve self-esteem by helping people to stay fit, look good, makes them strong and to give them a sense of achievement
2 People who exercise probably have a longer life expectancy.
3 It's written for adults. The word *adult* appears several times in the text. There are also references in the text to adult activities like having a job.

Exercise 7 page 109

1 *Answers will vary.*
2 *Answers will vary.*
3 *Possible answers:* People can become dehydrated or get injured. Some people become addicted to exercise.

READING 2

Exercise 1 page 109

1 balanced diet   2 junk food   3 Obesity   4 portions
5 campaign   6 nutritional

Exercise 2 page 110

Answers will vary.

Exercise 3 page 110

1 a 50%
  b 30%
  c 5%
  d 15%
2 laws for packaging, require restaurants to inform customers of calories, tax high-fat/high sugar foods

Exercise 4 page 110

a 3   b 2   c 3   d 1   e 4   f 5

Exercise 5 page 110

Possible answers:

2 to show more clearly how good or bad for you a particular food product is
3 to make junk food too expensive for people to buy in large quantities
4 to better protect children from the influence of junk food advertising
5 to encourage people to eat five portions of fruit and vegetables per day, to exercise, and to discourage them from eating fats and sugars

Exercise 6 page 112

1 rice, potatoes, pasta
2 milk, cheese
3 meat, fish, eggs, beans
4 candy, cookies
5 pizza, potato chips
6 chocolate, candy

Exercise 7 page 112

Possible answers:

1 The number of obese people has doubled over the last 25 years. Almost 70% of Americans are obese or overweight.
2 *Answers will vary.*
3 If people see that a food contains too much sugar, fat, or salt, they may choose to eat less of it or to not eat it at all.
4 The Malaysian government probably did research on the effects of junk food ads on kids. The research probably showed that the ads had a negative influence on children's food choices.

Exercise 8 page 112

Answers will vary.

LANGUAGE DEVELOPMENT

Exercise 1 page 113

We need to see a <u>reduction</u> in the rate of obesity among young people. The first step is <u>recognition</u> that fat is a real problem for young people. One solution is for schools to offer children the opportunity to participate in sports. This would require the involvement and <u>encouragement</u> of parents, who are our main weapon against increasing obesity. Parents can also support the <u>promotion</u> of educational campaigns to teach children about healthy eating. All of us should be responsible for the <u>protection</u> of our own health, but governments can also help fight the obesity epidemic. For example, they can impose a <u>ban</u> on junk food <u>advertisements</u> that target children.

Exercise 2 page 114

Obesity can reduce <u>life expectancy</u> and lead to <u>serious illness</u> such as <u>heart disease</u> and diabetes. To address this problem, some governments run <u>educational programs</u> and <u>advertising campaigns</u>. These educate people about the dangers of <u>junk food</u> and the importance of a <u>balanced diet</u>. They also show people how to find out about the <u>nutritional value</u> of food. Another important way to tackle obesity is <u>regular exercise</u>, because the more <u>physical activity</u> we have, the better we feel.

Exercise 3 page 114

2 nutritional value
3 educational programs
4 heart disease
5 physical activity
6 advertising campaigns
7 serious illness
8 balanced diet
9 regular exercise
10 junk food

CRITICAL THINKING

Exercise 1 page 115

argument 1: Individuals need to do their part to make sure they stay healthy.	evidence: individuals should eat smaller portions and a balanced diet
argument 2: Governments around the world must also do their part to fight obesity in their countries.	evidence: some countries provide nutritional information on food and on restaurant menus; some countries tax unhealthy food
argument 3: The role of the media and advertising should not be overlooked.	evidence: advertising junk food to children on TV was banned in Malaysia; there have been educational campaigns to encourage people to eat five portions of fruit and vegetables per day

Exercise 2 page 115
Possible answers:
arguments in favor
Exercise improves students' physical and mental health, which can benefit their studies.
It helps promote healthier lifestyles throughout a lifetime.
arguments against
Students are busy, and physical education classes will take time away from their studies.
Exercise is too expensive for some students.
Students should not be forced to take nonacademic classes.
Students are adults and responsible for their own health choices.

Exercise 3 page 116
Answers will vary.

Exercise 4 page 116
Answers will vary.

GRAMMAR FOR WRITING

Exercise 1 page 117
Possible answers:
1 In my opinion, governments should not pay for people to enroll in weight reduction programs.
2 I believe junk food advertisements should be illegal.
3 In my view, running is not the best exercise for keeping in shape.
4 I think most adults spend too much time sitting.
5 In my opinion, it's not necessary to sleep eight hours a night to stay healthy.

Exercise 2 page 118
Possible answers:
1 shouldn't
2 ought to
3 need to
4 don't need to
5 must

Exercise 3 page 118
1 to / in order to
2 so / so that
3 so / so that
4 to / in order to
5 so / so that

ACADEMIC WRITING SKILLS

Exercise 1 page 119
Possible answers:

1	**Introductory paragraph** **Topic:** *obesity* **Background:** *facts about obesity*
	Thesis statement / author's opinion: *Tackling obesity is the resp. of individuals, gov., and media*
2	**Topic sentence:** Indiv. need to do their part **Supporting detail:** *eat smaller portions* **Supporting detail:** eat a balanced diet
3	**Topic sentence:** Govs. must also do their part **Supporting detail:** food packaging show nutritional info **Supporting detail:** *restaurants list calorie counts* **Supporting detail:** tax on junk food

4	**Topic sentence:** Role of media & advert. **Supporting detail:** Advert. junk food forbidden in Malaysia **Supporting detail:** Educational campaigns on TV
5	**Concluding paragraph** **Restatement of thesis:** Indiv., gov., & media must do their part **Prediction or recommendation:** If all do their part, we may see the end of obesity in future

WRITING TASK

Exercise 1 page 120
Answers will vary.

Exercise 2 page 120
Answers will vary.

Exercise 3 page 121
Answers will vary.

Exercise 4 page 121
Answers will vary.

Exercise 5 page 121
Answers will vary.

Exercise 6 page 121
Answers will vary.

ON CAMPUS

Exercise 1 page 122
Answers will vary.

Exercise 2 page 122
1 d 2 b 3 a 4 c

Exercise 3 page 122
1 c 2 c 3 a 4 b

Exercise 4 page 123
Answers will vary.

Exercise 5 page 123
Answers will vary.

Exercise 6 page 123
Answers will vary.

Exercise 7 page 123
Answers will vary.

UNIT 6
ACTIVATE YOUR KNOWLEDGE
page 125
Answers will vary.

WATCH AND LISTEN

Exercise 1 page 126
Answers will vary.

Exercise 2 page 126
1 China
2–3 *Answers will vary.*

Exercise 3 page 127
Possible answers:
1 They live in cities in the north.
2 Most people live in the north, but the water is in the south.
3 Each section is built separately.
4 Because each section has to be in the perfect position
5 2030
6 It will help millions of people in the north.

Exercise 4 page 127
1 ~~food~~ water   2 ~~lake~~ river / canal   3 ~~570~~ 750
4 ~~12~~ 1200   5 ~~higher~~ lower   6 ~~2020~~ 2030

Exercise 5 page 127
Answers will vary.

READING 1

Exercise 1 page 128
1 harmful   2 helpful   3 prevent   4 pattern
5 unlimited   6 essential   7 illustrate

Exercise 2 page 128
1 *Possible answers*: biology, biography, biomedical, bioengineering
2 *Possible answers*: to copy (mimic), to copy from nature (biomimicry)
3 *Answers will vary.*

Exercise 3 page 130
c

Exercise 4 page 130
1 Velcro®, Speedo Fastskin® swimsuit, Eagle Eyes sunglasses, Bionic Car
2 burdock seeds, shark skin, eagle and falcon eyes, boxfish

Exercise 5 page 130
1 hooks and loops
2 children's clothing, lunch bags, shoes
3 Fastskin® fabric
4 swim faster
5 astronauts'

6 yellow oil
7 strength and low weight
8 the shape of the boxfish

Exercise 6 page 130
Possible answers:
1 It replaces buttons, zippers, and shoelaces, so it's easier for children to get dressed by themselves.
2 It was argued that suits made of Fastskin® gave some swimmers an unfair advantage.
3 Some people might think that it is ugly. Others might find it cute.

Exercise 7 page 131
Answers will vary.

READING 2

Exercise 1 page 131
1 power
2 personal
3 electronic
4 Three-dimensional
5 movement
6 breaks down
7 objects
8 Artificial

Exercise 2 page 132
Possible answers:
1 A Slovakian company plans to start selling flying cars from 2017.
2 A 3D printer is a printer attached to a computer than can make solid objects from a digital model by printing many separate layers of the object. It is used in manufacturing to print models, to print novelty food, to print low cost artificial limbs, etc.
3 Robots can help people who are missing arms or legs by providing artificial arms and legs that help people to have normal function such as picking things up.

Exercise 3 page 132
1 4 2 2 3 3

Exercise 4 page 132

invention	advantages	disadvantages
flying car	b	d
3D printing	f	a
robot suit	c	e

Exercise 5 page 134
1 T
2 F; Mechanical failure could be a serious problem for flying cars.
3 T
4 DNS

5 F; BMW and Volkswagen are already using 3D printing.
6 DNS
7 T

Exercise 6 page 134
Possible answers:
1 All machines have the potential to break down, and a breakdown in the air might cause falling objects that would be a serious danger below.
2 If everyone has a personal flying car and uses it like people use the roads today, then there will be air congestion.
3 They could help people do heavy or dangerous work.
4 Your arm could break.

Exercise 7 page 134
Answers will vary.

LANGUAGE DEVELOPMENT

Exercise 1 page 135
1 will definitely
2 probably won't
3 will probably
4 will probably
5 will definitely
6 definitely won't
7 could possibly

Exercise 2 page 135
1 In years to come
2 before the end of the decade
3 In the near future
4 before too long
5 within the next ten years
6 within two years
7 by 2020

Exercise 3 page 136
Possible answers:

de-	deactivate, defrost, degenerate
dis-	disengage, disobey, disappear
en-	enrage, endanger, enrich
pre-	prepare, predict
re-	reread, rewrite, replay
trans-	transfer, translate, transcribe
un-	uncertain, unbelievable, unfair

Exercise 4 page 136
1 same   2 same   3 opposite   4 same   5 opposite
6 opposite   7 same

Exercise 5 page 136
Answers will vary.

CRITICAL THINKING

Exercise 1 page 137

invention	advantages	disadvantages
flying car	3D freedom of movement	• traffic control • mechanical failure • air traffic congestion
3D printer	• make life size models • print body parts	slow
Ironman suit	• lift heavy objects • walk long distances • punch through walls • military uses • help people with disabilities	• expensive • short battery life • could injure wearer if badly programmed

Exercise 2 page 138
Possible answers:

home	solar roof, low-flush toilet, living walls, stand-up desk
space	Space X, Mars rovers, international space station
transportation	microcars, e-bikes, boosted skateboards
entertainment	HD TV, Bluetooth, smart watch, 3D glasses
computers	tablet computers, mobile apps
agriculture	drip irrigation, genetically engineered seeds, cage-free eggs

Exercise 3 page 138
Answers will vary.

GRAMMAR FOR WRITING

Exercise 1 page 139
Possible answers:
1 Scientists have already developed new robots that are able to do dangerous work.
2 There is a great deal of technology to help elderly people who may have trouble doing some tasks by themselves.
3 There is a huge amount of new investment in biofuels, which are cleaner and more sustainable than fossil fuels.

4 The Bionic Car has a special design that makes it more fuel efficient.
5 Important research is being done by scientists at the University of Cambridge, who hope to publish it next year.

Exercise 2 page 140

positive arguments	negative arguments
1, 5, 8, 9	2, 3, 4, 6, 7, 10, 11

Exercise 3 page 140
Possible answers:
1 The main advantage of
2 The main worry about
3 A real benefit of
4 The main disadvantage of
5 One bad thing about

ACADEMIC WRITING SKILLS

Exercise 1 page 141
1 The hook is the first two sentences. The word "However" gets the reader's attention.
2 The background information consists of definitions.
3 The topic is the influence of biomimicry. The point of view is that it can be seen in many everyday products. We don't know how many paragraphs there will be, but each paragraph will probably discuss a different product.

Exercise 2 page 142
1 The hook is a question: "What will the world of the future be like?"
2 The background information consists of two opposing views about the role of technology.
3 The topic is predictions. The point of view is "here are three." We know there will be three body paragraphs, and each one will discuss a different predictions.
4 The second introduction is better. It has a better hook, and the thesis statement gives a clearer idea about the number of body paragraphs.

WRITING TASK

Exercise 1 page 142
Answers will vary.

Exercise 2 page 142
Answers will vary.

Exercise 3 page 142
Answers will vary.

Exercise 4 page 143
Answers will vary.

Exercise 5 page 143
Answers will vary.

Exercise 6 page 143
Answers will vary.

Exercise 7 page 143
Answers will vary.

Exercise 8 page 143
Answers will vary.

Exercise 9 page 143
Answers will vary.

Exercise 10 page 143
Answers will vary.

Exercise 11 page 143
Answers will vary.

ON CAMPUS

Exercise 1 page 144
Answers will vary.

Exercise 2 page 145
1 T; Imagine you have a test that covers three chapters. You've already read the chapters but you don't have time to read them again. If the text is annotated, you can quickly review the most important points.
2 F; Use a pencil in case you want to make changes.
3 F; Use a system that you like.
4 T; Write your own ideas or opinions in the margin.
5 T; Write a short summary at the end of a section or chapter.

Exercise 3 page 145
1 example   2 definition   3 key word   4 effect
5 question   6 causes

Exercise 4 page 145
Possible answers:
1 There are three predictions: flying cars, home 3D printers and robot suits. These should be marked by underlining them and putting a star in the margin as they are the main ideas of the text.
2 The important details are the advantages and disadvantages of flying cars. These could be marked with + and – for each advantage/disadvantage or symbols, abbreviations, or words to explain why details are important
3 Examples are "Car companies like BMW and Volkswagen already use 3D printers to make life-size models of car parts" and "medical technology companies have already used 3D printing to make body parts, such as artificial ears." These should be marked with "ex" for "example" in the margin.
4 A definition in paragraph 4 is "exoskeleton". This should be marked in the margin as "def".

UNIT 7
ACTIVATE YOUR KNOWLEDGE
page 147
Answers will vary.

WATCH AND LISTEN

Exercise 1 page 148
Answers will vary.

Exercise 2 page 148
Possible answers:
1 The fashion industry
2 By hand
3 To work / To a formal occasion

Exercise 3 page 149
a 3   b 6   c 2   d 1   e 5   f 4

Exercise 4 page 149
jacket, pants, shirt, tie

Exercise 5 page 149
Possible answers:
1 Formal clothes. The designer talks about his father wearing formal clothes to mow the lawn and how people now look like they're dressed to mow the lawn for work.
2 No. The designer makes clothes by hand so can't make them in large numbers.
3 He doesn't like the way young people dress because he thinks it's too informal.
4 He want his clients to step out of their comfort zone by trying styles that they wouldn't normally wear.

Exercise 6 page 149
Answers will vary.

READING 1

Exercise 1 page 150
a season
b manufacture
c volume
d collection
e cotton
f invest
g brand

Exercise 2 page 150
Answers will vary.

Exercise 3 page 150
Possible answers:
1 Inexpensive clothing that is sold briefly in stores and then replaced with other styles.

2 In some shops they change daily or weekly. More expensive brands usually only have a new collection each season.

3 Frequent style changes make shoppers want to buy more. This can have a positive effect on the economy.

Exercise 4 page 152

a 4   b 2   c X   d 1   e 3

Exercise 5 page 153

2 ~~High-end fashion~~ Fast fashion designs that are unpopular are withdrawn in less than a month.

3 ~~Traditional~~ Fast fashion is good for the manufacturer because of the greater volume of sales.

4 The biggest problem with fast fashion is ~~theft of ideas~~ the impact of wasted clothes on the environment.

5 Cotton growers need to produce more, so they have to use ~~less~~ more fertilizer.

6 Designer clothing is popular with ~~middle-class~~ wealthy shoppers.

Exercise 6 page 153

1 Ahmet

2 Carmen

3 Sara

4 Fatima; Many people agree with her opinion about protecting the earth.

5 Jasmine; People dislike her wasteful attitude.

Exercise 7 page 153

Answers will vary.

READING 2

Exercise 1 page 154

1 multinational

2 wages

3 conditions

4 textiles

5 outsource

6 offshore

7 import

Exercise 2 page 154

Possible answers:

1 because labor costs are lower and, often, environmental regulations aren't as strict

2 Multinational companies bring jobs to local workers. Workers pay taxes, and this enriches the country.

3 Sometimes working conditions are bad.

Exercise 3 page 155

1 using offshore production to keep costs down in the textile industry

2 The writer is against it. In the thesis statement, the writer says that she thinks outsourcing is harmful.

Exercise 4 page 156

1 definition of outsourcing

2 overseas wages

3 working conditions in overseas factories

4 benefits of outsourcing to local economies; improving social conditions

Exercise 5 page 156

1 $122 billion

2 Multinational

3 40

4 don't exist or are ignored

5 117

6 economist

Exercise 6 page 157

1 fact

2 writer's opinion

3 fact

4 fact

5 fact

6 writer's opinion

Exercise 7 page 157

Answers will vary.

LANGUAGE DEVELOPMENT

Exercise 1 page 158

a supplier

b label

c overseas

d consumers

e advertising

f competitors

g labor

h manufacturing

CRITICAL THINKING

Exercise 1 page 159

Possible answers:

main argument Outsourcing is harmful for two reasons
reason 1 Overseas workers receive low wages **evidence:**   1 workers work 14 hours/day, earn < $100 / mo.   2 workers in 15 countries earn only 40% of money they need each month.   3 workers paid by piece, earn only a few cents per item that sells for 100s of $ in U.S., Europe   4 Priya Kapoor quote

> **reason 2** Working conditions overseas uncomfortable and unsafe
> **evidence:**
> 5 Worker protection laws don't exist or aren't followed
> 6 Workers exposed to chemicals, dust, etc.
> 7 Noise—author in Bangladesh 2015
> 8 Buildings unsafe
> 9 fire in Dhaka
>
> **concluding paragraph:**
> **evidence:** 10 Paul Krugman says outsourcing helps local economies.
> **final comment**: Multinationals. should share profits and improve social conditions overseas

Exercise 2 page 159
Answers will vary.

Exercise 3 page 160
facts: 3, 5, 6, 8
statistics: 1, 2
expert opinion: 10
quotations: 4
examples: 9
personal experience: 7

Exercise 4 page 160
1 Facts were used the most in Reading 2.
2–3 *Answers will vary.*

Exercise 5 page 160
Answers will vary.

Exercise 6 page 160
Answers will vary.

Exercise 7 page 160
Answers will vary.

GRAMMAR FOR WRITING

Exercise 1 page 161
1 instead of gerund
2 due to noun phrase
3 because of noun phrase
4 in spite of noun
5 along with noun

Exercise 2 page 161
1 in addition to
2 instead of
3 Other than / Apart from
4 Due to / As a result of
5 rather than

Exercise 3 page 162
1 Instead of
2 In addition to
3 In spite of
4 except for
5 along with

ACADEMIC WRITING SKILLS

Exercise 1 page 162
Body paragraph 1 b

Exercise 2 page 163
Within the fashion industry, some magazines and designers have recently begun promoting a more positive and realistic body image in their products.

Exercise 3 page 163
example: leading fashion magazine encouraging healthier approach to body image
example: companies using realistic models
quote: Pierre Dupont

Exercise 4 page 163
Answers will vary.

Exercise 5 page 163
1 Traditionally—transitions between ideas
  fashion designers—synonym for fashion industry
  one—pronoun referring to clothing collections
  Nowadays—transitions between sentences or ideas
  in contrast—transition between ideas
  they—fashion industry
2 the same outfits—synonym for sets of clothes
  This—refers to earlier idea
  clothing—repetition of noun
  Furthermore, transition between ideas
  so quickly—refers to earlier idea
  and—transition between ideas
  that—refers to earlier idea

Exercise 6 page 164
1 this
2 change
3 them
4 ones
5 they
6 This
7 that
8 In addition
9 these
10 Meanwhile

WRITING TASK

Exercise 1 page 164
Answers will vary.

Exercise 2 page 164
Answers will vary.

Exercise 3 page 165
Answers will vary.

Exercise 4 page 165
Answers will vary.

Exercise 5 page 165
Answers will vary.

Exercise 6 page 165
Answers will vary.

ON CAMPUS

Exercise 1 page 166
Answers will vary.

Exercise 2 page 167
1 e 2 c 3 a 4 d 5 b

Exercise 3 page 167
Possible answers:
1 Reliable
  Why: Website ends in .gov. Both authors are academics. It's from 2012 but not much is likely to have changed. There is an affiliation to a government scientific center. The audience is college level and above.
2 May be unreliable (needs more investigation)
  Why: Website ends in .com. No date is given. The author is an investigative journalist and author and not an academic. There is an affiliation to an institute for investigative journalism.
3 Unreliable
  Why: Website ends in .com. The author is a child. There is no affiliation so may just be opinion. The audience is children.

Exercise 4 page 167
Answers will vary.

Exercise 5 page 167
Answers will vary.

UNIT 8
ACTIVATE YOUR KNOWLEDGE
page 169
Answers will vary.

WATCH AND LISTEN

Exercise 1 page 170
Possible answers:
1 New York City, London, Tokyo
2 *Possible answers*: People lose their jobs / People don't have money
3 *Answers will vary.*

Exercise 2 page 170
Answers will vary.

Exercise 3 page 170
1 New York
2 October 29, 1929
3 It was the beginning of the Great Depression, where stock prices fell.
4 Banks, companies, people who lost their jobs.

Exercise 4 page 171
1 c 2 e 3 d 4 a 5 b

Exercise 5 page 171
Possible answers:
1 October 29, 1929
2 Millions of people
3 They fell 90%.
4 You can learn about the stock market crash.
5 Computers and electronic boards

Exercise 6 page 171
Possible answers:
1 Yes
2 Because the economies of countries are connected. The US lent money to Europe after World War I and when the US economy collapsed money stopped being sent to Europe and economies in European countries collapsed as well, resulting in job losses.
3 Computers let people get information quickly. More people can get stock information with computers.

Exercise 7 page 171
Answers will vary.

READING 1

Exercise 1 page 172
a interest rate
b return
c stocks and shares
d investor
e value
f recession
g investment

Exercise 2 page 172
1 *Possible answers*: stocks, bonds, real estate, gold, jewels, coins, art
2 *Answers will vary.*
3 *Answers will vary.*

Exercise 3 page 174
two popular investments, the price of gold over time, classic cars as an investment, the risks of investing

Exercise 4 page 174
Paragraph 1: popular investments
Paragraph 2: the price of gold over time
Paragraph 3: classic cars as an investment
Paragraph 4: the risks of investing

Exercise 5 page 174

1 $283 an ounce
2 the price doubled
3 $1661 an ounce in 2012
4 the price will remain about the same
5 $13,000
6 $1 million
7 $4.1 million

Exercise 6 page 174
Possible answers:

1 the stock market
2 classic cars
3 Yes; because it costs money to keep them in excellent condition, and because investors have to guess which car is going to become valuable

Exercise 7 page 175
Answers will vary.

READING 2

Exercise 1 page 175

a savings
b standard of living
c factor
d expenditure
e income
f percentage

Exercise 2 page 176
Answers will vary.

Exercise 3 page 176

1 The standard of living is worse in the United States now than it was twenty years ago.
2 income, number of people in family, costs for rent, utilities, food, medical bills, education, etc.

Exercise 4 page 176
Answers will vary.

Exercise 5 page 176

b

Exercise 6 page 176

1 b
2 a
3 b
4 b
5 a

Exercise 7 page 178
Possible answers:

1 Because they are nonessential expenditures
2 The rising cost of oil; higher prices for cars; higher prices for public transportation; people living farther from their place of employment, and thus spending more to commute
3 $13,400 (25% of income)

Exercise 8 page 178

1 less because wages have decreased and expenditure has increased
2 probably not, because the stock market is risky
3 *Answers will vary.*

LANGUAGE DEVELOPMENT

Exercise 1 page 178
Possible answers:

economy (n) the system by which a country produces and uses goods and money
finance (n) the control of how large amounts of money should be spent
wealth (n) a large amount of money or valuable possessions that someone has
poverty (n) the state of being very poor
value (n) how much money something could be sold for
employment (n) paid work that someone does for a person or company
profession (n) a type of work that needs special training or education
expense (n) the money that you spend on something economic
financial (adj) relating to money or how money is managed
wealthy (adj) rich
poor (adj) having very little money or few possessions
valuable (adj) valuable objects could be sold for a lot of money
employed (adj) working for a company that pays you a wage
professional (adj) relating to a job that needs special training or education
expensive (adj) costing a lot of money

Exercise 2 page 179

1 economy
2 financial
3 wealthy
4 poverty
5 valuable
6 employment
7 Professional
8 expensive

Exercise 3 page 179

1 market
2 purchase
3 consumers
4 trend
5 demand
6 Revenue
7 supply

CRITICAL THINKING

Exercise 1 page 180

1 Median expenditures in five categories as a percentage of income
2 percentages
3 1996–2014
4 There are five categories of expenditures: housing (dark red); food (pink); transportation (green); pets, toys, and entertainment (blue); and health (red)
5 10%
6 decrease
7 Prices for housing, food, and transportation started to rise. Prices for pets/toys/entertainment and healthcare stayed the same until 2013, when they also began to rise.

Exercise 2 page 181

1 Between 1996 and 2004, expenditures as a percentage of income generally went down for housing, food, and transportation. In 2004 these same categories started to get more expensive. There are many possible reasons for this change. Housing prices go up when there aren't enough affordable houses and apartments. Transportation costs go up when the price of oil increases or people live farther from their places of employment. Food prices are affected by the weather. For example, in years when there is not enough rain, food becomes more expensive.
2 Housing. Housing costs are affected by availability, bank interest rates, changes in the stock market, and global events. Housing prices are very sensitive to changes in any of these factors.
3 Pets, toys, and entertainment. These are nonessential items. They are a small part of most people's budget.
4 The percentage that Americans spent on all categories went up. This trend is probably part of the normal rise and fall in prices.
5 It is lower than it was in 1996.

Exercise 3 page 182

1 Physical home video (orange line) = DVD. Electronic home video (blue line) = movies / TV shows that can be downloaded or streamed.
2 2010 to 2019
3 The numbers represent millions of dollars. The largest dollar amounts are at the top.
4 2014

Exercise 4 page 182

1 16 million   2 5 million   3 2019

Exercise 5 page 182

1 1 electronic home videos 2 physical home videos
2 Reasons could include the loss of physical stores as customers have moved more and more to online shopping; also, improved computer processing speeds have enabled high quality downloads, so people are more motivated to download videos and watch them at home.

GRAMMAR FOR WRITING

Exercise 1 page 183

1 a   2 f   3 d   4 c   5 b   6 e

Exercise 2 page 183

2 a dramatic fall
3 a slight decrease
4 a gradual increase
5 a considerable fluctuation

Exercise 3 page 184

1 from; to; of
2 from; to; of
3 From; to; from; to
4 between; and
5 from; to

Exercise 4 page 184

1 nearly
2 over
3 around; about; approximately
4 under

Exercise 5 page 184

1 g   2 d   3 e   4 a   5 c   6 b   7 f

ACADEMIC WRITING SKILLS

Exercise 1 page 185

1 ... the combination of rising prices and falling incomes has left many Americans with less spending power than they had twenty years ago.
2 In conclusion
3 b, d

WRITING TASK

Exercise 1 page 186
Answers will vary.

Exercise 2 page 186
Answers will vary.

Exercise 3 page 186
Answers will vary.

Exercise 4 page 186
Answers will vary.

Exercise 5 page 186
Answers will vary.

Exercise 6 page 186
Answers will vary.

Exercise 7 page 186
Answers will vary.

Exercise 8 page 187
Answers will vary.

Exercise 9 page 187
Answers will vary.

ON CAMPUS

Exercise 1 page 188
Answers will vary.

Exercise 2 page 189
1 T
2 DNS
3 T
4 F; You will need to get the transcript translated.

Exercise 3 page 189
Answers will vary.

Exercise 4 page 189
Answers will vary.

Exercise 5 page 189
Answers will vary.

UNIT 1

▶ **Great Egret and Dolphin Fishing Teamwork**

The marshes of South Carolina are the location of an interesting fish tale.

There, these dolphins and egrets work together in a very special way.

These egrets are experts on the dolphins' behavior.

The moment a dolphin comes to the surface of the water and checks the nearest mud bank, the birds get ready for action.

Then, it happens. The dolphins push the fish onto the shore.

When the fish are out of the water, the dolphins start eating. But the egrets also join them for dinner.

This is the only place in the world where you can see this kind of behavior.

Strangely, the dolphins always use their right sides to push the fish to the shore.

The young dolphins learn this fishing technique from their parents, and so do the young egrets. Many of the birds now depend on the dolphins for their food. They never even fish for themselves. These egrets and dolphins demonstrate the ability of different animal species to work together in order to survive.

UNIT 2

▶ **Colorado River, Grand Canyon, Yosemite**

Some of the world's most beautiful natural environments are in the southwestern United States.

In just a few million years, the Colorado River has cut through parts of Arizona to form the Grand Canyon.

The Grand Canyon is 277 miles long and, in some places, 18 miles wide. At its deepest places, the river is a mile below the top of the canyon. It shows the effects of water and weather on the Earth's surface.

Its oldest rocks are almost 2 billion years old, nearly half the age of the Earth. This is the world's largest canyon, and the weather here can change dramatically. In the same day you can have hot, dry weather, followed by wind and snow. And every year the Colorado River cuts a little deeper into the bottom of the Grand Canyon.

Water also formed Carlsbad Caverns in New Mexico. Carlsbad is the largest, deepest cave system in North America. Even today water continues to change the inside of the caves.

The results are spectacular.

Finally, high in the Sierra Mountains of California is Yosemite National Park. Its famous landmark Half Dome was made by the frozen water in a glacier moving through the canyon. Today the glaciers are gone, but water from the melting mountain snow flows throughout the national park.

Yosemite Falls drops nearly 2,500 feet—it's the tallest waterfall in North America.

UNIT 3

▶ The Jumbo Jet

Narrator: In 1969, a true giant of the skies first took flight. It could cross the Atlantic with enough fuel and twice as many passengers as any airplane before it. Now, there are nearly 1,000 of them. Each one is able to fly over 14 hours to their destinations without stopping. It's the 747—the jumbo jet—and this is the very first one.

Jimmy Barber helped build this very plane.

Jimmy Barber: Eight months straight you worked on the airplane, and we didn't just work, err, eight hours a day. Sometimes we worked 12 or more hours a day. And if it was necessary to sleep in your car in a parking lot, that's what you did. It was a highlight in my whole life was this aircraft, you know. Yeah.

Wow, this is great.

Narrator: This is the first time Jimmy has been aboard since he worked on it over 45 years ago.

Jimmy Barber: This is great.

Narrator: When it first flew, this was the most modern plane in the air. It was the first double-decker jet in history with a fancy first-class lounge upstairs.

Jimmy Barber: And the upper deck, one airline turned that into a disco and put a dance floor up there. Another airline put piano bars in his ... in these airplanes.

Narrator: But it was the enormous space downstairs that changed commercial air travel forever. With room for around 500 people, it started the age of low-cost air travel.

Since its first flight, engineers have redesigned the 747 fifteen times. Today it flies further and faster than ever before.

UNIT 4

▶ Halloween by the Numbers

Now, a little Halloween by the numbers. Tens of millions of trick-or-treaters are expected to hit the streets tomorrow. We purchase an estimated 600 million pounds of candy for Halloween, and if you haven't gotten to it yet, we are told that the most popular variety is—no surprise—chocolate. Other top costume choices include witches, pirates, and Batman. More than a billion pounds of pumpkins were grown last year. Illinois is the nation's number one pumpkin producing state. As for the origin of trick-or-treating, it is thought to have evolved from a Celtic tradition of putting out treats to placate the spirits who roam the streets during a sacred festival that marked the end of the Celtic year. Finally, you may be surprised to learn that there is nothing frightening about Halloween if you are a retailer. It is the second highest grossing holiday after Christmas. The National Retail Federation estimates the average person will spend nearly $75 on decorations, costumes and, of course, candy.

UNIT 5

▶ Nutrition Labels

Reporter: Today the Food and Drug Administration proposed a food label makeover. Jeff Pegues tells us it includes a reality check that some feel is long overdue.

Jeff Pegues: What and how people eat have changed. Now, for the first time in two decades, the labels on foods will change, too. The calories will be featured more prominently, and any added sugars or sweeteners will be listed as well. FDA commissioner Margaret Hamburg.

Margaret Hamburg: We're also asking for a change in serving size to reflect the realities of what people are eating.

Jeff Pegues: Here's what that means. The label on this pint of Ben & Jerry's chocolate chip cookie dough ice cream says each half-cup serving has 280 calories and 25% of the fat we should eat every day. Under the FDA proposal, the serving size would be a more realistic cup, which means each serving would contain 560 calories and 50% fat. At least publically, the food and beverage industry has been supportive. The Grocery Manufacturers Association says it's critical that any changes ultimately serve to inform and not confuse consumers. Some beverage companies, like PepsiCo, have already made changes, but what may be difficult for the industry to swallow, the overall price tag.

A senior Obama administration official says the cost of implementing the changes could reach 2 billion dollars. First Lady Michelle Obama is a driving force behind the new labels.

Michelle Obama: As consumers and as parents, we have a right to understand what's in the food we're feeding our families, because that's really the only way that we can make informed choices.

Reporter: This is just a proposal, so there will be a public comment period. Nora, the FDA says it may be two years before consumers see these new labels on food in stores.

UNIT 6

▶ China's Man-made River

History is filled with stories of humans overcoming obstacles through discovery and invention. Take an enormous country like China. What do you do when most of your people live in the north, in cities like Beijing, but most of your water is in the south? You build an artificial river to bring water from the south to the north.

This river will be about 750 miles long when it is finished in 2030.

And this is it. A giant raised canal, or aqueduct—one of the largest engineering projects in the world.

Chinese workers and engineers are building the river piece by piece, in separate sections.

Each section starts as a metal framework.

A team of 20 people build the metal frame.

Then the concrete is added.

Finally, the section is moved into place using one of the world's most powerful cranes.

Each section weighs 1,200 tons—more than three commercial airplanes.

This woman operates the crane. It's a very important job, and it takes great skill.

She must work very carefully so that each section of the artificial river is in the perfect position.

The water will flow north to Beijing without using any pumps.

So the end of each section must be exactly 1 centimeter lower than the other end.

When the river is finished and operating in 2030, the water from the south will reach millions of Chinese people in the north.

UNIT 7

 A Life Tailored Around Clothes

Edgar Pomeroy: I'm Edgar Pomeroy. I grew up in Savannah, Georgia, and I knew I wanted to be a fashion designer when I was ten years old. Well, every day I used to watch my father get dressed because I would be watching cartoons or something on TV in their bedroom. And he was always putting on pinstripe suits and polka-dot ties and waistcoats and dressed to the nines, as they say. He was the only one I've ever known to mow the lawn in a Brooks Brothers button-down and khaki pants, and Weejuns, might I add. That's really how it all began.

Father: But you've always been able to put fabrics and colors together.

Edgar Pomeroy: Yeah, but look who I'm talking to. We're bespoke tailors as well as I'm more of a designer so we make our shirts and suits and all our clothes right here. We don't source anything out.

This is for a client that I'm seeing tomorrow.

All the stripes match. The plaids come down. This is detail.

I'm upstairs when I'm in town pretty much all the time, checking the jackets and pants and seeing who's doing what. It has to fit. You can do the most beautiful cloth in the world but if you botch the cutting, it's over. It's just another piece of cloth that should be burned up in the floor. It got very lackadaisical in the 90s when the dot-com era came into play. And I was kind of disappointed because people kind of started dressing way down. Some even looked like they just mowed their lawn. I dress people who love clothes. People who want to stand out, elegantly, of course. But they're dandies.

I didn't want to overkill this because you're conservative.

I go to their houses in Chicago, I go to L.A., I go to Baltimore, New York, London. I go all over. You know, I build a trust with them and I design for them. What I do is get to know their personality. If I go to their office or home, I look around, I see how it's decorated, I look at pictures, and I design around their personality. But I want them to take a little bit of a step out of their comfort zone. A little one, just to try. I let the client have the stage. I just kind of help them get to the stage.

UNIT 8

▶ Stock Market Crash of 1929

Narrator: On October 29, 1929, the New York Stock Exchange had its worst day ever—Black Tuesday. The stock market crashed, and investors lost billions of dollars in a single day. That day was the end of a decade of a strong U.S economy. It was the beginning of the Great Depression, the worst economic period in modern world history. During the next two years, stock prices fell 90%, banks and companies failed, and millions of people around the world lost their jobs.

Today you can visit the Museum of Financial History on Wall Street, in New York City, to learn more about what happened.

Man: So what we have here is the physical tape from October 29th, that Black Tuesday, and it's quite an important piece, it tells a great story.

Narrator: This is a replica of the machine that produced that ticker tape. The name *ticker tape* comes from the sound of the machine as it printed out the price of stocks and shares. But since the early 1970s, computers and electronic boards have reported the ups and downs in the stock market.

Name: _____ Date: _____

Read the article. Then, answer the questions that follow.

1   The Portuguese man-of-war got its name because it looks like a war ship on the water's surface. It is also as dangerous as one. Some people think it is a jellyfish, but this sea creature is actually a group of tiny animals working together. The Portuguese man-of-war prefers warm waters such as the tropical parts of the oceans, which are good sources of food. They float in groups, sometimes with more than 1,000 men-of-war. They cannot swim on their own, so they float wherever the wind or the sea takes them.

2   Although the man-of-war floats on the surface, its tentacles are under the water. The tentacles are the long, thin parts of its body that it uses to get food. The tentacles help the man-of-war **survive**. They can be up to 165 feet (50 meters) long. Each of these tentacles has poison, which the man-of-war uses to kill fish and other small sea creatures that swim into its tentacles. In fact, even when it is dead, this creature can still sting. Whereas the sting is **fatal** for most fish, it rarely is for humans, but it is extremely painful.

3   **Common** signs that you have been stung are a feeling of burning and a redness of the skin. If you are stung, you should take the following steps. First, remove any parts of the tentacles that may be stuck to your skin. Be careful not to touch them with your fingers. Then, apply salt water or fresh water. You can also apply heat or cold to help the pain. People who have more serious reactions should see a doctor.

PART A KEY SKILLS
READING FOR MAIN IDEAS

1 Circle the best title for the text.

   a Signs You've Been Stung   **b** A Dangerous Sea Creature   **c** Tropical Fish

2 Write the paragraph number next to the main ideas.

   a The tentacles of the Portuguese man-of-war _____
   b A general description of the Portuguese man-of-war _____
   c The sting of the Portuguese man-of-war _____

PART B ADDITIONAL SKILLS

3 Write *T* (true) or *F* (false) next to the statements. Correct the false statements.

   1 _____ The Portuguese man-of-war is not a jellyfish.
   _____

   2 _____ The Portuguese man-of-war swims in warm waters.
   _____

   3 _____ The tentacles can grow up to 50 feet long.
   _____

   4 _____ A dead Portuguese man-of-war is still dangerous.
   _____

   5 _____ The sting is often fatal to humans.
   _____

   6 _____ Fresh or salt water is a good way to help the pain of a Portuguese man-of-war's sting.
   _____

UNIT 1 LANGUAGE QUIZ

Name: _____ Date: _____

PART A KEY VOCABULARY

1 Choose the correct word to complete each sentence.

1 The burning of fossil fuels is a _____ cause of air pollution. It caused 70% of all air pollution in the U.S. in 2014.
   a major   **b** fatal

2 Other causes of air pollution, such as smoke from forest fires and volcanoes, are _____ .
   a native   **b** natural

3 _____ used in farming and cleaning are harmful when they get into the air.
   a Species   **b** Chemicals

4 Air pollution can cause lung _____ , which makes it difficult for a person to breathe.
   a disease   **b** chemical

5 Smoking can be _____ . It leads to more than 480,000 deaths per year in the U.S.
   a common   **b** fatal

6 _____ increases in air pollution, more and more people in the town are becoming sick.
   a Major   **b** Due to

7 It is important to use clean energy that does not _____ the air.
   a pollute   **b** protect

8 Humans are not the only ones who suffer from air pollution. Animal and plant _____ are affected too.
   a species   **b** diseases

9 A _____ sign of a sick plant is yellow leaves. You can often see this in cities and in forests.
   a common   **b** cruel

2 Complete the paragraph with the correct form of the words in the box.

> cruel   destroy   endangered   native   protect   survive

> Animals that are (1) _____ are disappearing from our world. Why are they dying? Why can they not (2) _____ ? In some cases, people (3) _____ their habitats by cutting down trees to use the land. Then the animals have nowhere to live. In these cases, the plants that are (4) _____ to the habitat are also affected. They can no longer grow. This means that if we can (5) _____ a habitat, we can help both the plants and animals there. It is (6) _____ to think that the world is just for humans. We need to share the earth with plants and animals, and not hurt them.

PART B LANGUAGE DEVELOPMENT
ACADEMIC VERBS

3 Choose the correct verb to complete each sentence.

1 Some animals use chemicals to communicate. They _____ a chemical when there is danger to let other animals know.
   a release   **b** contrast

2 Air pollution _____ our water. The pollution mixes with rain and gets into rivers, lakes, and oceans.
   a cooperates   **b** affects

3 Some seeds _____ themselves to animal fur or bird feathers. Then they are carried to other places and grow there.
   a release   **b** attach

4 Many animals _____ to survive. They work in groups to hunt or protect themselves from other animals.
   a cooperate   **b** attach

5 In my presentation, I will compare and _____ animals that work together to hunt and animals that hunt alone.
   a contrast   **b** cooperate

COMPARATIVE ADJECTIVES

4 Complete the sentences using the comparative form.

1 *Whale sharks do not attack humans, whereas tiger sharks have attacked 111 humans since records began.*
Tiger sharks are _____ (dangerous) whale sharks.

2 *The tiger shark is not at risk of extinction, whereas the whale shark is endangered.*
The tiger shark is _____ (common) the whale shark.

3 *Whale sharks do not have sharp teeth or a powerful bite, unlike tiger sharks.*
A tiger shark's bite is _____ (strong) a whale shark's.

4 *The red squirrel has a typical head-and-body length of 7.5 to 9 inches, whereas the gray squirrel has a typical head-and-body length of 9 and 12 inches.*
The gray squirrel is _____ (large) the red squirrel.

5 *Gray squirrels weigh more than red squirrels.*
Gray squirrels are _____ (heavy) red squirrels.

Name: _____ Date: _____

PART A GRAMMAR FOR WRITING
WORD ORDER

1 Rewrite the words in the correct order.

1 lives / in warm waters / The Portuguese man-of-war / .

_____

2 it / on the beach / can also be found / However, / .

_____

3 very dangerous / are / Portuguese men-of war / to humans / .

_____

4 use / their tentacles / They / for stinging / .

_____

5 eats / fish / The Portuguese man-of-war / other sea creatures / and / .

_____

COMBINING SENTENCES

2 Circle the correct word to complete the sentence.

1 *Neither / Both* the red squirrel and the gray squirrel have long tails.
2 *Neither / Both* the red squirrel nor the gray squirrel lives on the Isle of Man.
3 The gray squirrel is common, *but / and* the red squirrel is not.
4 *Both / Neither* the red squirrel and the grey squirrel can bite humans when they are angry.
5 Lions *or / and* tigers are two types of wild cats.
6 House cats eat plants and animals, *whereas / and* wild cats eat only meat.
7 House cats can live in the country *and / but* the city. They don't need a lot of space.
8 House cats are usually not dangerous, *whereas / and* wild cats are very dangerous.
9 Lions do not live in North *and / or* South America. Their home is in the forests of India and parts of Africa.
10 Wild cats eat meat *or / but* they usually do not eat fish.

PART B WRITING TASK

> Compare and contrast a Portuguese man-of-war and a jellyfish.

3 Read the information in the chart. Write two paragraphs about the similarities and differences of the two ocean species.

	Portuguese man-of-war	Jellyfish
Habitat	Oceans (prefers warm waters such as the tropical parts of the oceans)	All ocean waters (very cold to very warm waters) and in fresh water
Length	Tentacles up to 165 feet long	Tentacles up to 120 feet long
Diet	Fish and other sea creatures	Plankton (plants)
Behavior to humans	Some stings can be fatal.	Some sting. Most are harmless to humans.

Name: _____ Date: _____

Read the article. Then, answer the questions that follow.

The Consequences of Climate Change on Glaciers

1 Glaciers are important to our world. They cover about 10% of earth and hold 75% of the world's fresh water. These huge moving masses of ice start as snow, turn to ice, and eventually crash into the sea.

2 Across the globe glaciers are melting, leading to an increase in water and a rise in sea levels. Melting mountain glaciers are responsible for one-third of the increase in sea levels. Twenty-five percent of that increase is from Alaska's mountain glaciers, which are melting because of climate change. In fact, for the past 19 years, 75 billion tons of water pour into the sea from the melting glaciers in Alaska every year.

3 To better understand the impact of climate change on Alaska's glaciers, scientists have followed the streams that run through these slowly disappearing mountains of ice. These fast rivers of freezing water are formed as glaciers melt and are an important measure of the health of a glacier. Every glacier is in a careful balance. The amount of snow falling in winter must equal the amount that melts in the summer. If that balance changes, and there is less snow than the amount that melts in the summer, the glacier will begin to disappear. Right now, that is what is happening. These glaciers are melting faster than they are growing, and when a glacier disappears, it is gone for good.

4 As the glaciers melt, the rise in sea level threatens our world's ecosystems. Already, many of the world's islands are in danger of flooding. In addition, fish and other sea life depend on water temperatures which are also changing. The effects of global warming threaten human and animal life. We cannot predict the future, but we know the consequences of climate change are serious.

PART A KEY SKILLS
READING FOR DETAILS

1 Read the article again and complete the chart with supporting details.

Definition of glaciers	a
Percentage of the world's fresh water in glaciers	b
Percentage of increase in sea level from Alaska's melting glaciers	c
Reason glaciers disappear	d
Example of the effects of climate change on an ecosystem	e

PART B ADDITIONAL SKILLS

2 Complete the sentences with the correct form of the words or numbers in the box.

| grow   ice   melt   rise   snow   1/3   19   25   75 |

1 If glaciers continue to melt, the sea level will continue to _____ .
2 When temperatures increase, glaciers _____ .
3 Glaciers begin as snow and then turn into _____ .
4 The amount of _____ in winter must equal the amount that melts in summer for glaciers to be healthy.
5 Alaskan glaciers are melting faster than they are _____ .
6 Glaciers hold _____ % of the world's fresh water.
7 Water from melting mountain glaciers account for _____ of the increase in the sea levels.
8 The percentage of the melting mountain glaciers that Alaska is responsible for is _____ %.
9 Every year 75 _____ tons of water melt into the sea from glaciers in Alaska.
10 The amount of water from melting glaciers in Alaska has been the same every year for _____ years.

Name: _____   Date: _____

PART A KEY VOCABULARY

1 Match the sentence halves.

1 The **destruction** of forests leads to _____	a carbon dioxide and give off oxygen.
2 The **climate** is _____	b breathing problems.
3 The **cause** of melting glaciers is _____	c more flooding due to fewer trees.
4 One **effect** of air pollution on people is _____	d increasing temperatures.
5 **Farming** is _____	e the weather in an area over a long period of time.
6 An **ecosystem** is _____	f oil, which is found in the earth.
7 An example of a **fossil fuel** is _____	g the use of land to grow food and raise animals.
8 Trees **absorb** _____	h the process of building houses, schools, and other structures.
9 **Construction** is _____	i the plants and animals in an area and their effect on each other and the environment.

2 Complete the paragraph with the correct form of the words in the box.

atmosphere   greenhouse gas   global warming   logging   rainforest   threaten

(1) _____ destroys land, and the consequences of cutting down trees are serious. First, this often happens in the (2) _____ , which have some of the world's most diverse species of plants growing in this wet climate. The plants and animals that live in this area are (3) _____ as their homes are destroyed. In addition, this practice contributes to the problem of (4) _____ and rising temperatures. Because the trees are no longer there to absorb carbon dioxide, it goes into the (5) _____ , and is added to other (6) _____ , like methane.

PART B LANGUAGE DEVELOPMENT
ACADEMIC VOCABULARY

3 Complete the sentences with the correct form of the word or phrase from the box.

annual   challenge   contribute to   predict   trend

1 Many human behaviors, like burning fossil fuels, _____ climate change.
2 Weather reporters _____ temperatures and weather patterns using advanced equipment.
3 The _____ rainfall in California has fallen for the past five years.
4 One _____ we can see in the last ten years is more people sharing cars and riding together.
5 Many of the environmental _____ we face are problems that humans created.

ENVIRONMENT COLLOCATIONS

4 Complete the sentences with the correct form of the words in the box.

climate   environmental   greenhouse   plant   tropical

1 Power _____ often burn fossil fuels to produce electricity.
2 The increase in _____ gases in the atmosphere is one of the main causes of global warming.
3 Most scientists agree that human activity is a major cause of today's _____ change.
4 The largest _____ rainforest is the Amazon Basin in South America.
5 Many _____ groups, like the Sierra Club and Audubon Society, raise money to protect plants and animals.

Name: _____ Date: _____

PART A GRAMMAR FOR WRITING
VERBS OF CAUSE AND EFFECT

1 Put the words in the correct order to make sentences.

1 erosion and problems / with the soil / Destruction / leads to / of forests / .

_____

2 is / Climate change / human behavior / the result of / .

_____

3 are / melting glaciers / Flooding and changes / in sea level / caused by / .

_____

4 results / Burning fossil fuels / in carbon dioxide / an increase / in / .

_____

5 due to / Warmer temperatures / are / climate change / .

_____

BECAUSE AND *BECAUSE OF*

2 Circle the correct word to complete the sentence.

1 A loss of biodiversity is dangerous *because / because of* it reduces new sources of food and medicine.
2 Islands may flood *because / because of* rising sea levels.
3 Demand for food and energy is expected to rise *because / because of* the increase in the population.
4 The climate is changing *because / because of* human activity.
5 Carbon emissions are rising *because / because of* humans are burning fossil fuels.

PART B WRITING TASK

What is the world's biggest environmental problem today? Describe its causes and effects.

3 Write two paragraphs. In the first paragraph discuss the causes, and in the second paragraph discuss the effects.

Name: _____ Date: _____

PART A KEY SKILLS
PREDICTING CONTENT USING VISUALS

1 Look at the photos in the reading, and write *T* (true) or *F* (false) next to the statements.

_____ 1 The text will discuss ways people commute.
_____ 2 The text will only describe modern types of transportation.
_____ 3 The text will mainly focus on one type of transportation.

Read the article. Then, answer the questions that follow.

Transportation in India

1 India has a population of 1.2 billion. However, only 6% of households own cars. How do so many people in this growing country get to their destinations each day?

2 One form of traditional Indian transportation is the water taxi. These boats carry thousands of passengers along the Ganges River every day. Another way to travel is by ox cart, traditionally used in the outskirts of cities and in the countryside of India. Some cities have banned ox carts and other slow moving vehicles on the main roads to reduce traffic congestion. Bicycles are also very popular in India, and more than 60% of households own at least one. But while such private modes of transportation are useful, India's public transportation systems are among the most heavily used in the world.

3 Fifty-three of India's cities have a population of over one million people, so the public transportation system is essential for urban life. The main forms of public transportation are small motor vehicles, buses, and railroads. Rickshaws, a type of small, bicycle-powered taxi, are common, too. Although some of these cities have bus systems, many people use smaller road vehicles, which results in some of the worst traffic problems in the world.

4 The railways are another popular form of public transportation. They were first introduced to India in 1853. In 1951, the many different systems were nationalized into one system, becoming one of the largest rail networks in the world. Now Indian trains carry over 23 million passengers daily. While Indian trains are safe and generally efficient, they often run late, but are still preferable to spending hours in traffic. However, with India's growing population, unless more public transportation is offered, it may not be possible to avoid long commutes.

PART B ADDITIONAL SKILLS

2 Complete the table using words from the article.

Traditional transportation	(4) _____ transportation
(1) _____ carry commuters along the river.	Motor vehicles, buses, and (5) _____ are used in cities.
(2) _____ are used in the countryside but are not allowed in some cities.	(6) _____ are small, bicycle-powered vehicles.
More than 60% of households own (3) _____ .	Indian (7) _____ carry over 23 million passengers daily.

3 Check the statements that the author would agree with.

1 India needs more public transportation options. ☐
2 Traditional forms of transportation are the best ways to get around. ☐
3 Taking the train is better than driving in traffic in India. ☐
4 More people in India should buy cars. ☐
5 Big cities need many modes of public transportation. ☐

Name: _____ Date: _____

PART A KEY VOCABULARY

1 Complete the paragraph with the correct form of the words in the box.

commuter congestion connect government outskirts practical rail vehicle

The city council is meeting to discuss traffic [(1)] _____ , especially during rush hour. Cars and other [(2)] _____ move very slowly at this time, and reports of road rage and accidents are increasing. One solution is to expand the [(3)] _____ system so that it reaches more areas outside the city. By extending train service to the surrounding areas and city [(4)] _____ , we can decrease the number of people on the roads by increasing the number of [(5)] _____ on the train. The purpose of today's meeting is to determine if this is a [(6)] _____ solution, considering the city's financial budget. We will be reviewing the costs involved in order to [(7)] _____ the outer areas of the city to the downtown. The city [(8)] _____ will make its decision in November.

2 Match the questions and answers.

1 Do you take **public transportation**? _____
2 Does your city have lanes for **cycling**? _____
3 Is an **emergency** causing this slow traffic? _____
4 Do you need more **fuel** for the car? _____
5 Is your **destination** downtown? _____
6 Do you work in **engineering**? _____

a No, bikes have to ride in the street with cars.
b Yes, I design bridges.
c Yes, I ride the bus to work.
d No, it's just normal rush hour delays.
e Yes, I have to get some gas soon.
f No, I'm traveling outside the city today.

PART B LANGUAGE DEVELOPMENT
TRANSPORTATION COLLOCATIONS

3 Match the words to make collocations about transportation.

1 bike _____
2 car _____
3 parking _____
4 public _____
5 road _____
6 rush _____
7 traffic _____

a congestion
b hour
c lane
d rage
e restrictions
f pool
g transportation

4 Complete the sentences with collocations from Exercise 3. You will not use all of the collocations.

1 The new rail system will carry 310,000 passengers daily, decreasing _____ on the road and air pollution caused by cars.
2 I use the _____ that runs along the river when I cycle to work.
3 The _____ here is very unreliable. The trains and buses are always late.
4 There are _____ between 8am and 6pm, so do not leave your car on the street during the day.
5 The angry man almost hit me with his car in a moment of _____ .

SYNONYMS FOR VERBS

5 Replace the words in bold with academic synonyms in the box. You will not use all the synonyms.

attempt   consider   convince   prevent   produce   reduce   require   waste

1 I don't think you can **get** people to travel by bus if they want to drive. _____
2 The government must **think about** transportation options for areas outside the city center. _____
3 Cameras will not **stop** further accidents. We need to lower speed limits. _____
4 We do not **need** any more investment in public transportation. _____
5 It would be difficult to **try** to force people to take trains instead of cars to work. _____

Name: _____ Date: _____

PART A GRAMMAR FOR WRITING
FUTURE REAL CONDITIONALS

1 Put the words in the correct order to make sentences.

1 we will increase / traffic on the river / we / If / add / more water taxis, / .

   _____

2 rail commuters / will get angry / the number of trains, / reduce / we / If / .

   _____

3 the city / will have / tests vehicle emissions, / If / we / better air / .

   _____

4 increase / If / we / fewer young people / the driving age, / will have accidents / .

   _____

5 If / the city / will cycle / more people / of bike lanes, / increases the number / .

   _____

IF ... NOT AND UNLESS

2 Complete the sentences using *if, not,* or *unless.*

1 The railway system will not improve _____ we build better trains.
2 _____ we do _____ use cleaner transportation, then pollution will not be reduced.
3 _____ we act now, it will be too late.
4 We will _____ solve the traffic problem _____ we build houses closer to the business areas.

PART B WRITING TASK

> What problem could building bike lanes solve?

3 Write three paragraphs. In the first paragraph, write about the problem and discuss the advantages of bike lanes. In the second paragraph, discuss the disadvantages of bike lanes. In the third paragraph, write a conclusion, and include your opinion about adding bike lanes.

Name: _____ Date: _____

Read the article. Then, answer the questions that follow.

The Morris Dance: An English Tradition

1   From the samba in Brazil to the halay in Turkey, traditional dances are part of the culture and history of many countries. One such dance in England is the morris dance. Morris dancing, also known simply as "morris," is a type of English folk dance traditionally associated with the month of May and the spring season. It is performed outdoors, usually by trained groups of women or men. However, the exact origins and history of the dance are unclear. Although some people think it can be traced to the 14th century, others point to its appearance in Shakespeare's plays in the 17th century. Finally, it is others' belief that the name comes from the Moors of North Africa.

2   No matter its origin, morris dancing is very lively. The dancers often have bells on their knees that ring loudly as they dance. The dancers are usually arranged either in two lines or in a circle facing each other. They wear different clothes, depending on which part of England they are from. Whatever their particular costume, male morris dancers usually wear white shirts with colored bands around their chests. They often wave white handkerchiefs or carry short sticks that they bang together as they dance.

3   Morris dances have a long tradition, but the dance also changes with the times. Some morris groups can trace their roots back over 150 years. More recently, morris groups have attempted new dances based on contemporary themes. In April 2012, a Wiltshire morris dance group created a series of dances that mimic the world's heaviest flying bird, the Great Bustard. This bird was hunted to extinction in the United Kingdom in 1832, but was reintroduced to Wiltshire, England in 2004. This new dance series was invented to raise British awareness of the Bustard.

PART A KEY SKILLS
ANNOTATING

1   Follow the directions to annotate the reading.

1   Underline the topic sentence in each paragraph.
2   Circle the month the morris dance is associated with.
3   Number the three different beliefs of the dance's origins.

4   Box another word for *special clothes* in Paragraph 2.
5   Put two lines under a detail that supports the idea that the morris dance is very lively.
6   Box a synonym for *create* in Paragraph 3.

PART B ADDITIONAL SKILLS

2   Choose the correct answers to complete the sentences.

1   The samba is a _____ .
   a   Brazilian dance   b   Turkish dance
2   The author wrote the article in order to _____ .
   a   explain how to perform the morris dance
   b   explain how the dance connects to culture.
3   Another word for *origin* is _____ .
   a   beginning   b   place

4   The history of the morris dance has _____ .
   a   different stories   b   one story
5   The information about the Wiltshire morris dance group supports the idea that _____ .
   a   the morris dance is an ancient tradition
   b   the morris dance shows modern ideas

UNIT 4 LANGUAGE QUIZ

Name: _____ Date: _____

PART A KEY VOCABULARY

1 Choose the correct words that can replace the words or phrases in bold in the sentences.

1 At a job interview, **how you look** is very important.
   a your appearance   **b** your relationship
2 When I **meet** someone in the street, I usually smile and shake hands.
   a greet   **b** exchange
3 My husband and I **give each other** gifts on our wedding anniversary.
   a expect   **b** exchange
4 My favorite picture is a photo from Thanksgiving with all my **family members**.
   a relatives   **b** couples
5 A common **topic** in the news is climate change and its effect on the environment.
   a culture   **b** theme
6 It's my **thought** that everyone should read the news and be aware of what's happening in the world.
   a relationship   **b** belief
7 There was a wonderful **party** after the wedding, and people danced late into the night.
   a reception   **b** ceremony
8 I **think** that traditional dances will continue to be an important part of our culture.
   a appear   **b** expect

2 Complete the paragraphs with the correct form of the words in the box.

ceremony   couple   culture   engaged   formal   relationship

We use different words to discuss our ⁽¹⁾ _____ with people. For example, most languages have words for family members and relatives. In English, there are different terms to talk about a man and a woman as a(n) ⁽²⁾ _____ . In the beginning, we use the words *boyfriend* and *girlfriend*. Then when two people get ⁽³⁾ _____ , we call the man *fiancé* and the woman *fiancée* until they get married.

The wedding is considered a very special occasion. Many people invite their closest friends and family to the wedding ⁽⁴⁾ _____ . Although different ⁽⁵⁾ _____ around the world have different wedding traditions, in most countries the bride and groom dress in ⁽⁶⁾ _____ clothes as a way to show respect for such an important event.

PART B LANGUAGE DEVELOPMENT
AVOIDING GENERALIZATIONS

3 Read the generalizations. Use the words in parentheses to make the sentences more accurate.

1 Everyone in the United States loves football. (many people)

_____

2 Couples have receptions after their wedding ceremonies. (usually)

_____

3 German speakers are always more direct than English speakers. (tend)

_____

4 Couples expect you to fly to a vacation destination for their wedding. (occasionally)

_____

5 Americans always dress informally. (tend)

_____

6 The Japanese culture is quite formal. (can)

_____

7 People give speeches and congratulate newlyweds at the reception. (normally)

_____

8 When you visit someone's house for the first time, you are expected to bring a gift. (frequently)

_____

9 In India, people think it is impolite to say "no." (many)

_____

10 Couples do not have a wedding celebration with friends or relatives. (sometimes)

_____

SYNONYMS TO AVOID REPETITION

4 Choose the correct synonyms from the box to replace the words in bold. You will not use all the words.

brief   certain   common   important   obvious   separate   serious

1 People in **powerful** government positions can have a lot of influence on laws. _____

2 It was not **clear** how long the ceremony would last, but we knew it would not be short. _____

3 We had a **short** stop in Dallas before flying to Mexico City. _____

4 It is **usual** for a newly married couple to go on a honeymoon. _____

5 In **some** countries, people often get married when they are over thirty. _____

UNIT 4 WRITING QUIZ

Name: _____   Date: _____

PART A GRAMMAR FOR WRITING
PARAPHRASING

1 Read the original sentence and its paraphrase. Which strategy or strategies did the writer use to paraphrase? Write *I* for indirect speech, *S* for synonyms, and *W* for changing word order.

> "The morris dance is actually older than we think. The word *moris* is Latin and means 'tradition'." Source: Eudora Walter
>
> Paraphrase: According to Eudora Walter, *moris* is a Latin word, meaning "tradition," and the morris dance has an even older history than we are aware of. _____

2 Use the strategies in parentheses to paraphrase the sentences.

1 Morris dancing, also known simply as "morris," is a type of English folk dance traditionally associated with the month of May and the spring season. (use synonyms; change word order)

_____
_____
_____

2 More recently, morris groups have attempted new dances based on contemporary themes. (use synonyms; change word order)

_____
_____
_____

3 "I've been watching morris dancing for years and it's always exciting, but the Wiltshire morris dance representing the Great Bustard communicated an important message." Source: Jonathan Milton (use indirect speech and synonyms)

_____
_____
_____

PART B WRITING TASK

> Summarize and respond to "The Morris Dance: An English Tradition."

3 Write a summary paragraph of the text in the Unit 4 Reading Quiz. Then write a response paragraph, and include your opinion about traditional dances.

Name: _____ Date: _____

Read the article. Then, answer the questions that follow.

Training the Body to Race

1 The best of the world's road cyclists ride in races which take them over 2,100 miles (3,500 kilometers) at an average speed of 28 miles per hour (45 kilometers per hour) on flat roads. How is this amazing physical achievement possible?

2 Teams who compete in the world's toughest road cycle races, like the Tour de France, credit their success to training. The riders set goals for each day's training. They also recognize the need to take regular breaks. This means that even though cyclists in training average about 770 miles (1,240 kilometers) a week, they do not train so hard that they get injured before their race.

3 Cyclists are more in shape than normal people. The best riders get twice as much oxygen from each breath as an average healthy person, so they are able to generate twice as much energy. Due to the riders' intense physical exercise, their hearts also pump blood to their muscles much faster than those of most people.

4 Naturally, because cyclists are so active, they need to eat a lot of calories. They pay attention to the nutritional value of their calories. Cyclists burn fat by not eating too many carbohydrates. However, in a race they need more calories for energy. During the Tour de France, a cyclist can consume up to 8,000 calories per day. In comparison, the average person's recommended daily amount is just 2,000 calories.

5 This kind of physical training and focus is essential in order to win a race, especially a long distance race such as the Tour de France, which takes 23 days, including only two days of rest. As a result cyclists must take their preparation seriously. Even the smallest aspect of a rider's performance could make the difference between winning and losing.

PART A KEY SKILLS
MAKING INFERENCES

1 Read the sentences. Check the boxes next to the statements that the author would agree with.

   1 Cyclists who race in the Tour de France are putting their bodies in serious danger. ☐
   2 Long-distance cyclists are in better health than the average person. ☐
   3 The average person is overweight. ☐
   4 Competing in the Tour de France is something most people can do. ☐
   5 Diet is an important part of being a serious cyclist. ☐

PART B ADDITIONAL SKILLS

2 Complete the sentences with details from the article.

   1 Most serious cyclists train by riding _____ miles a week.
   2 On flat roads, the average cyclist in a long-distance race travels _____ miles per hour.
   3 In comparison to the average healthy person, a cyclist takes in more _____ to produce more energy.
   4 Cyclists pump more _____ to their muscles.
   5 A cyclist doesn't eat too many carbohydrates and, as a result, he or she reduces _____ .

Name: _____   Date: _____

PART A KEY VOCABULARY

1 Complete the paragraph with the correct form of the words in the box.

| active   balanced diet   campaign   junk food   moderate   obesity   recognize   self-esteem |

Educational programs in schools and advertising [1] _____ on the Internet and TV have been successful. The message is clear. Exercising and being more [2] _____ during the day makes people feel better. It can even improve people's moods and [3] _____ . In fact, research shows that even [4] _____ exercise, like going for a ten-minute walk, can make a difference in how we feel. This habit, combined with a(n) [5] _____ with lots of fruits and vegetables, leads to healthier lifestyles. However, although the message is out, three out of four men in the United States are overweight or suffer from [6] _____ . In my opinion, this is partly because healthy foods are often expensive, whereas fast food and [7] _____ are usually cheaper. We must [8] _____ that we have to make healthy foods available to everyone. We have to change both our exercise and eating habits if we want to be healthy.

2 Choose the correct words from the box to complete the sentences.

| calorie   nutritional   portion   reduce   serious |

1 If you look at the _____ value that is posted on food labels, you might be surprised.
2 Many foods have labels that say they are low in _____ , so people think the food is better for them.
3 You should always look at the _____ on food labels. For example, pasta labels often show a serving size of half a cup, but most people eat at least a full cup.
4 If you want to lose weight, you have to _____ the number of calories you eat.
5 There can be _____ effects to overeating. Weight gain leads to physical problems and disease.

PART B LANGUAGE DEVELOPMENT
VERB AND NOUN FORMS

3 Cross out one mistake in a verb or noun form in each sentence, and write the correct form.

1 We must recognition the seriousness of the disease so we can better solve the problem of obesity. _____
2 We need to do more than reduction our calories to be healthy. _____
3 It is the responsibility of parents to encouragement their children to eat healthy foods. _____
4 Another thing we can change is how people look in advertise. _____
5 If we promotion healthy bodies on TV, people will feel better about themselves. _____

HEALTH AND FITNESS COLLOCATIONS

4 Match the sentence halves.

1 Around the world, life _____   a exercise sleep better.
2 People should pay attention to the nutritional _____   b disease are an effect of healthier eating.
3 Reductions in heart _____   c activity includes walking.
4 Physical _____   d value of the foods they buy.
5 People who get regular _____   e expectancy is increasing.

Name: _____ Date: _____

PART A GRAMMAR FOR WRITING
STATING OPINIONS

1 Read the questions and answer them with the opinion phrases in parentheses.

1 Should children eat junk food? (In my view)

_____

2 Should people buy organic fruits and vegetables? (In my opinion)

_____

3 Do people need to exercise every day to be healthy? (I think)

_____

4 Is it the government's job to keep people healthy? (I believe)

_____

5 Do most people get enough sleep? (In my opinion)

_____

STATING A PURPOSE

2 Circle the correct answer to complete the sentence.

1 People should make dinner at home *so / in order to* they can limit their portion sizes.
2 People ought to run with friends *so / to* make exercise more fun.
3 Children should have gym class every day *so that / in order to* they can get more physical activity.
4 People should not eat candy and junk food *so / to* they can reduce the sugar they eat.
5 Parents should model good eating habits *in order to / so that* show children a healthy diet.

PART B WRITING TASK

What habits make someone healthy?

3 Write an opinion essay. Include an introductory paragraph, two body paragraphs, and a concluding paragraph.

Name: _____ Date: _____

Read the essay. Then, answer the questions that follow.

How Are Robots Like Us?

1   Robots are widely used today in factories, in space, and deep under water for jobs that are too dirty, boring, or dangerous for humans to do. Robots are also increasingly common in the home. Robot vacuum cleaners, lawnmowers, and other such devices have become very popular in some countries. While these robots for the home are helpful, they are nothing compared with the human-like robot ASIMO.

2   ASIMO, which has been in development by Honda Motor Company since 1986, is one of the most advanced robots in the world. Honda wanted to build a robot that could move like a human with abilities to help out in the home, play sports, and even dance. Over the years there were some problems developing a robot with these advanced movements. However, researchers soon had a robot that could walk on uneven surfaces and climb stairs. They continued to improve the model, and now ASIMO can even move out of the way of objects in its path.

3   The robot is also designed to be people-friendly. ASIMO can push a cart, and open and close doors. It can also shake hands. Standing 5 feet 2 inches (158 centimeters) tall, ASIMO looks like a child wearing a spacesuit. Like a child, it can look into the faces of adults who are sitting down. Using a camera, it can recognize some faces. With these advancements, Honda thinks ASIMO will definitely be helpful, especially for elderly people at home or those who can't walk on their own or who have other disabilities.

4   Researchers are now working on robots that can learn about the world around them and respond to human touch and voice. One concern with these advanced robots is that they will take the jobs people need. However, the main advantage of these robots is that they can help people. They can complete work that could be harmful to humans, assist people in need, and do some of the tasks humans do not want to do.

PART A KEY READING SKILLS
SCANNING FOR INFORMATION

1   Read the questions. Scan the text for the underlined words, and answer the questions.

Question	Answer
1 What are two examples of <u>robots</u> commonly used <u>in the home</u>?	
2 What three <u>movements</u> did the researchers at <u>Honda</u> want <u>ASIMO</u> to do?	
3 How <u>tall</u> is <u>ASIMO</u>?	
4 What does <u>ASIMO</u> use to <u>recognize</u> <u>faces</u>?	
5 What is the <u>main advantage</u> of advanced <u>robots</u>?	

PART B ADDITIONAL SKILLS

2 Write *T* (true) or *F* (false) next to the statements. Correct the false statements.

_____ 1 Researchers at Honda Motor Company have been developing ASIMO since 1986.
_____

_____ 2 The author thinks ASIMO is similar to other robots people commonly use in the home.
_____

_____ 3 ASIMO can open doors for people.
_____

_____ 4 Researchers are improving robots so the robots can learn about the world and drive cars.
_____

_____ 5 People are worried that advanced robots will take their jobs.
_____

Name: _____   Date: _____

PART A KEY VOCABULARY

1 Read the sentences. Complete the sentences with synonyms from the box for the words in parentheses.

| artificial   essential   harmful   movement   pattern   power   prevent   unlimited |

1 Some chemicals for cleaning are _____ (dangerous) for humans to breathe.
2 If you want to be healthy, it is _____ (necessary) to eat well and exercise.
3 A runner's _____ (actions), such as taking small steps, are very important to winning a race.
4 Some of the world's _____ (energy) comes from burning coal and other fossil fuels.
5 If we want to _____ (stop) people from speeding, we should put cameras on all major roads.
6 There are many _____ (unnatural) flavors and chemicals in foods that are added to change their color or taste.
7 If you have the Internet, your access to knowledge is _____ (without end).
8 I use a(n) _____ (repeating set) of letters and numbers so I can more easily remember my password.

2 Match the questions to the answers.

1 Did your car **break down**? _____
2 Is the robot **helpful**? _____
3 Can I use an **electronic** signature? _____
4 Can you **illustrate** the meaning of *exoskeleton*? _____
5 Can the robot pick up **objects**? _____
6 Is this your **personal** car? _____
7 Can you give an example of a **three-dimensional** object? _____

a No, it belongs to my company.
b Yes, and it can pour a cup of coffee.
c Yes, think of a globe or a cube.
d Sure, I'll give you an example.
e Yes, it cleans the house.
f Yes, I need to find a ride.
g No, we ask people to use a real pen.

PART B LANGUAGE DEVELOPMENT
MAKING PREDICTIONS WITH MODALS AND ADVERBS OF CERTAINTY

3 Complete the sentences about the future using modal and adverb phrases with the meaning in parentheses.

1 Computers _____ be more powerful in the future. (100% yes)
2 People who don't smoke _____ live longer than those who do. (90% yes)
3 The managers _____ hire new workers later in the year, but it's hard to predict. (50% yes)
4 I _____ get the job because I couldn't answer all the questions on the interview, but I'll know for certain next week. (80% no)
5 We _____ be able to breathe in space without special equipment. (100% no)

PREFIXES

4 Match the words in the left column to the words or phrases in the right column with opposite meanings.

1 unsafe _____
2 prevent _____
3 disorganized _____
4 enlarge _____
5 decrease _____

a make bigger
b make smaller
c not dangerous
d make happen
e neat

Name: _____ Date: _____

GRAMMAR FOR WRITING
RELATIVE CLAUSES

1 Join each pair of sentences to make one sentence with a relative clause. Add commas if necessary.

1 One research study about robots involved a ten-year-old girl. She was given a robot doll for several weeks.
_____

2 The design manager has a favorite question. The question is about what robots will be like in the future.
_____

3 Most people choose to use an elevator instead of taking the stairs. An elevator is a kind of machine.
_____

4 I'm sending you an email I received from Max Mustermann. Max attended your webinar about robots.
_____

5 Please provide a short description. The description should include details of the design of your robot.
_____

PREPOSITIONAL PHRASES WITH ADVANTAGES AND DISADVANTAGES

2 Match the sentence halves.

1 A real benefit of advanced robots is _____
2 The main worry with advanced robots is _____
3 The main argument in favor of buying a new car is _____
4 One bad thing about buying a new car is _____
5 One point against using humans instead of robots is _____

a that it costs a lot of money.
b that they easily become bored.
c that they will take jobs people need.
d their ability to help humans in need.
e that it will have the latest technology.

PART B WRITING TASK

> What are the advantages and disadvantages of using advanced robots in the workplace?

3 Write an explanatory essay. Include an introductory paragraph, at least two body paragraphs, and a concluding paragraph.

Prism 2 Reading and Writing © Cambridge University Press 2017 **Photocopiable**

Name: _____ Date: _____

Read the article. Then, answer the questions that follow.

Blue Jeans: An American Tradition

1　Many inventions have shaped American culture. One was created many years ago but is still popular today: Levi's jeans. In my opinion, this invention is a very American story, involving an immigrant and his success.

2　Levi Strauss was born in 1829 in Bavaria, which is part of Germany today. Like many immigrants, he moved to America and settled in New York. In 1853, he moved from New York to San Francisco, where people were mining for gold. However, unlike many other hopeful travelers, Strauss didn't go to California to mine for gold. He saw a different opportunity. He became a supplier of clothes, boots, and other goods to small stores that sold these products to miners. This is how people become successful. They see a need and create a business. But this is not how Strauss made most of his money. It was through his work with Jacob Davis.

3　Davis made clothes for the many people in California who were doing hard labor, like gold mining. They needed pants that would last, so Davis used material from Strauss and added metal rivets to the pockets to prevent tearing. Davis asked Strauss to invest in the pants and Strauss saw another opportunity. Soon they were in business together. In 1873, blue jeans were for sale. As a result of the new design, demand for the product increased. Strauss opened a factory in San Francisco to manufacture the jeans and hired hundreds of workers. When he died in 1902, the company kept going.

4　By the 1920s, the miners had left California but other workers were buying Levi's. It became one of the leading brands in men's work clothing. In the 1950s, after movie stars Marlon Brando and James Dean were seen wearing them, jeans became a common item of clothing for all Americans. Today Levi's jeans are still one of the most popular products of American culture, and the Levi Strauss & Company is a multinational company with offices all over the world. Like many American inventions, I think blue jeans exist because of an immigrant's hard work and smart decisions.

PART A KEY SKILLS
DISTINGUISHING FACT FROM OPINION

1 Look at the sentences from the reading. Check whether they are facts or the writer's opinion.

		Fact	Opinion
1	In my opinion, this invention is a very American story, involving an immigrant and his success.		
2	In 1853, he moved from New York to San Francisco, where people were mining for gold.		
3	This is how people become successful. They see a need and create a business.		
4	Today Levi's jeans are still one of the most popular products of American culture, and the Levi Strauss & Company is a multinational company with offices all over the world.		
5	Like many American inventions, I think blue jeans exist because of an immigrant's hard work and smart decisions.		

PART B ADDITIONAL SKILLS

2 Number the events in the correct order.

    a Levi Strauss became a supplier of clothes, boots, and other goods to small stores. _____

    b Blue jeans were for sale. _____

    c People were mining for gold. _____

    d Levi Strauss & Company is a multinational company. _____

    e Davis asked Strauss to invest in the pants. _____

Name: _____   Date: _____

PART A KEY VOCABULARY

1 Complete the paragraph with the correct form of the words in the box.

conditions   invest   manufacture   offshore   outsource   volume   wage

In the United States, some people do not want to [1] _____ jobs to other countries. They want the jobs to stay at home, and yet many businesses have factories overseas. These businesses [2] _____ clothing, electronics, cars, and many other products in factories in other countries where they can pay workers less. Now, some people want to move those factories from [3] _____ locations back to the United States. However, I don't think it will work. Businesses are not going to pay the higher [4] _____ that American workers want. In addition, many of these businesses have already [5] _____ millions of dollars in their overseas production. They don't want to lose this money. I also don't think factories in the United States can match the [6] _____ that these overseas factories produce. There they employ millions of workers for long hours, while workers in the United States are used to jobs that last from 9a.m. to 5p.m. Finally, the working [7] _____ in the United States are generally much better but also more expensive than those for workers overseas. I'm afraid most of those manufacturing jobs have left the country for good.

2 Complete the sentences with the correct form of the words from the box that have the same meaning as the words or phrases in parentheses.

brand   collection   cotton   import   multinational   season   textile

1 What are your favorite clothing _____ (labels)?
2 Do you know how many people work in the _____ (fabric) industry worldwide?
3 What _____ (time of year) are most new fashions advertised in?
4 Did you buy clothes from any of the famous _____ (fashion house designs) this spring?
5 Many clothes are made from _____ (the soft cloth that is made from a plant) grown in China and India.
6 The United States _____ (buys from another country) many products from China, such as toys and clothes.
7 Some _____ (global) companies invest in the areas of the world where they have factories.

PART B LANGUAGE DEVELOPMENT
VOCABULARY FOR THE FASHION BUSINESS

3 Match the numbered sentences to the correct lettered sentences.

1 My neighbors sell sports equipment to small stores and businesses. _____
2 Human rights groups are concerned about the working conditions in factories. _____
3 Many consumers wait until a product has been for sale for a while before buying it. _____
4 Big chain stores are major competitors in the fashion business. _____
5 Many name brands use famous people in their advertising, and it works. _____

a For instance, many people in manufacturing are paid low wages and work in unhealthy environments.
b They can compete with the famous designers because their clothes often look like expensive brands but cost much less.
c As suppliers, they make money from the businesses that sell their goods.
d They think they can then get the product for a cheaper price.
e People buy the product so they can feel beautiful, talented, or strong, like the people they see.

Name: _____   Date: _____

PART A GRAMMAR FOR WRITING
MULTIWORD PREPOSITIONS

1 Complete the sentences with the correct words or phrases in the box.

| along   apart   due   except   in addition   instead   in spite   other   rather   result of |

1 _____ to longer hours, my new job will also mean extra responsibilities.
2 _____ with swimming, running is my favorite sport.
3 _____ than my gold watch, I don't own any expensive jewelry.
4 When possible, I prefer to take public transportation _____ than go by car.
5 I don't eat meat, _____ for fish and chicken.
6 _____ of my strong communication skills and experience, I didn't get the job.
7 I'd like to see a younger woman in a management position in our company _____ of just another old man in a gray suit.
8 He was disappointed as a _____ the news that he did not get the job.
9 _____ to my experience, I was chosen for a second interview. I hope I get the job!
10 I had no identification in my wallet, _____ from my gym membership card.

PART B WRITING TASK

> Fashion companies should never outsource their work to other countries. Do you agree or disagree?

2 Write an argumentative essay. Include an introductory paragraph with a thesis statement that states your opinion and arguments, two body paragraphs with supporting reasons and evidence, and a concluding paragraph that summarizes your position.

Name: _____   Date: _____

Read the article. Then, answer the questions that follow.

Healthy Economies, Healthy Societies

1   The citizens in countries ruled by democratic governments are used to regular elections. Governments change, but often it takes time before there is an effect on a country's economic growth. However, the situation can be different in countries ruled by people who are not voted into power.

2   When a government falls suddenly, the country's economy can experience major difficulties. Interest rates often rise, natural resources may not be protected, and the economy can suffer. This loss of wealth can lead to poverty and to a recession. One reason for this is a decrease in investment from overseas. A typical pattern follows: a country's leader falls, foreign investors leave, there is a sharp decrease in the market value of the money, people lose jobs, and business sales fall.

3   Despite this situation, many investors put their money into overseas financial institutions, which can offer high returns. However, they must be aware of the risks involved. Business people may benefit from high interest rates offered by banks overseas, but this model can often not be sustained, and people can lose huge amounts of money. This trend was seen in 2013 in Cyprus when banks increased their loans for housing, but then home prices fell rapidly.

4   Investors looking for a safer long-term return can invest in the economy of a country rather than simply saving their money in banks. Such investments can create jobs, develop new businesses, restaurants, and shopping malls in a country. Outside wealth can turn a country's failing economy around.

5   If businesses invest in long-term projects such as factories, mining, and other resources needed for manufacturing, a country's economy can improve. In addition, governments have a major role in the investment of money and resources in the country. Through government spending and taxation, their countries' economies can become more stable, and their societies can benefit as people gain access to healthcare, housing, and jobs.

PART A KEY SKILLS
SKIMMING

1   Skim the text. Check the topics that the text discusses.

   1   the rules for democratic elections ☐
   2   the effects on an economy when a government changes quickly ☐
   3   the risk involved with investing in overseas financial institutions ☐
   4   investment options for long-term growth ☐
   5   the government's responsibility in maintaining the economy ☐

PART B ADDITIONAL SKILLS

2 Complete the summary with the correct form of the words in the box. There is one extra word.

| business   sale   economy   election   interest   investment |
| manufacturing   natural resource   overseas   recession   standard of living |

Some countries hold regular (1) _____ and although there is a change in the government, the effects on the economy are not immediate. However, when a governments fails, a country's (2) _____ can suffer. When important (3) _____ such as coal, wood, and oil are not managed well, the economy can decline dramatically. When an economy suffers badly, the country can experience negative growth. This is known as a (4) _____ , and it usually includes the loss of jobs and can lead to poverty. This situation can happen when there is a sudden loss of (5) _____ coming from other countries. A drastic fall in the value of a country's money can lead to a decrease in (6) _____ because people can no longer afford the prices charged by stores. Some financial institutions offer high (7) _____ rates; however, investors risk losing a lot of money if the market fails. Money from investors can help foreign countries, especially when the money goes toward developing jobs and businesses in these (8) _____ countries. For instance, economies will become more stable if businesses invest in large projects such as those needed for the (9) _____ industry. The government is also important. It can direct money to the resources people need to improve their (10) _____ .

Name: _____   Date: _____

PART A KEY VOCABULARY

1 Match the answers to the questions.

1 Is the country in a **recession**? _____
2 Has your **standard of living** decreased? _____
3 Do you have much money in **savings**? _____
4 Do you own **stocks and shares**? _____
5 Do you spend a large **percentage** of your salary on rent? _____
6 Do you make a good **return** on your investments? _____
7 Do you pay a high **interest rate** on your car loan? _____
8 Did your **income** increase? _____

a Yes, I've been putting money in the bank since I was 15.
b Not really. I get about 3% annually from them.
c Yes, I got a 5% raise last year.
d Yes, 40% of my income goes to housing.
e No, I don't invest in the stock market.
f Yes, ten years ago I could afford more things.
g Yes, the bank charges me 10%.
h No, job growth is up, and the economy is doing well.

2 Write the correct form of the words in the box with the same meaning as the words or phrases in parentheses.

| expenditure   factor   investment   investor   value |

1 Did the _____ (worth) of your home go down in the recession?
2 What are the main _____ (reasons) that lead to a recession?
3 What _____ (money spent) do you have each month?
4 Do you know any _____ (people who put money into businesses) who can give me financial advice?
5 Buying property is usually a good _____ (way to make money).

PART B LANGUAGE DEVELOPMENT
NOUNS AND ADJECTIVES FOR ECONOMICS

3 Cross out the incorrect noun or adjective form in each sentences. Write the correct form.

1 The country has been in a poor finance state since the decline of the manufacturing industry. _____
2 We need to invest in programs that help poverty people. _____
3 Houses have fallen in valuable over the past few years. _____
4 This is the kind of investment our economic needs to avoid recession. _____
5 She could not find employed as an architect so she decided to go back to school. _____

NOUNS FOR ECONOMIC TRENDS

4 Complete the paragraph with the correct form of the words in the box.

| consumer   demand   market   purchase   trend |

In the last few years, more and more people have been buying homes. This [1] _____ is taking place in cities and in suburbs. As the [2] _____ for homes increases, home prices go up. Overall, this is good for the housing [3] _____ , which has had problems. In addition to home [4] _____ , research shows that people are making other big expenditures. As a result, the economy is improving as [5] _____ spend money.

Name: _____   Date: _____

PART A GRAMMAR FOR WRITING
DESCRIBING GRAPHS

Look at the graph about U.S Home Ownerships. Then, complete Exercises 1 and 2.

1 Choose the correct words to complete the paragraph about the graph.

> This graph shows there was *(1) a slight rise / rise slightly* in U.S. home ownership until 2005. While home ownership did not *(2) fall dramatically / dramatic fall*, the percentage of homeowners from 2005 to 2015 clearly *(3) decreased / increased*. Rather than showing considerable fluctuations, the graph shows that overall there was a *(4) slight increase / slight decrease* in homeownership in the first ten years and a *(5) gradual decrease / sharp decrease* in the next ten years.

Home Ownership in the United States

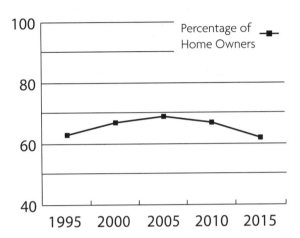

Source: Federal Reserve Bank of St. Louis
(https://fred.stlouisfed.org/series/RHORUSQ156N#0)

2 Use *from, to, and, of,* or *between* to complete the paragraph about the graph.

> *(1)* _____ 1995 to 2005, U.S. home ownership increased. *(2)* _____ 2005 and 2015, home ownership decreased. There was an increase *(3)* _____ 3% in home ownership between 1995 *(4)* _____ 2000. Overall, the percentage of U.S. home owners from 1995 *(5)* _____ 2015 decreased.

3 Match the phrases to the figures.

1 nearly twenty dollars _____   a $14.75
2 roughly twenty-five dollars _____   b $29.62
3 a little under fifteen dollars _____ c $25.18
4 a little more than fifteen dollars _____ d $19.50
5 approximately thirty dollars _____   e $15.28

PART B WRITING TASK

Describe the multiple line graph showing the sales revenue of two technology companies, and explain the data.

4 Write an analysis of the multiple line graph. Include an introductory paragraph, two body paragraphs, and a concluding paragraph. Describe the graph in the first body paragraph, and interpret the data in the second body paragraph.

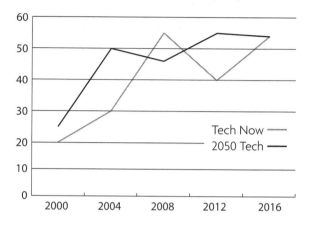

Technology Sales Revenue in Millions (US$)

Prism 2 Reading and Writing © Cambridge University Press 2017 **Photocopiable**

UNIT QUIZZES ANSWER KEY

UNIT 1 READING QUIZ
PART A KEY SKILLS

1 b

2 a 2   b 1   c 3

PART B ADDITIONAL SKILLS

3 1 T
2 F; The Portuguese man-of-war floats in warm waters. It cannot swim.
3 F; The tentacles can grow up to 165 feet (50 meters) long.
4 T
5 F; The sting is fatal for most fish, but it isn't usually fatal for humans.
6 T

UNIT 1 LANGUAGE QUIZ
PART A KEY VOCABULARY

1 1 a   2 b   3 b   4 a   5 b   6 b   7 a   8 a   9 a

2 1 endangered   2 survive   3 destroy   4 native
5 protect   6 cruel

PART B LANGUAGE DEVELOPMENT

3 1 a   2 b   3 b   4 a   5 a

4 1 more dangerous than   2 more common than
3 stronger than   4 larger than   5 heavier than

UNIT 1 WRITING QUIZ
PART A GRAMMAR FOR WRITING

1 1 The Portuguese man-of-war lives in warm waters.
2 However, it can also be found on the beach.
3 Portuguese men-of-war are very dangerous to humans.
4 They use their tentacles for stinging.
5 The Portuguese man-of-war eats fish and other sea creatures.

2 1 Both   2 Neither   3 but   4 Both   5 and
6 whereas   7 and   8 whereas   9 or   10 but

PART B WRITING TASK

3 *Answers will vary.*

UNIT 2 READING QUIZ
PART A KEY SKILLS

1 a huge moving masses of ice
b 75%
c 25%
d The glaciers melt faster than they grow.
e Fish and other sea life depend on water temperatures, which are changing. OR Many of the world's islands are in danger of flooding.

PART B ADDITIONAL SKILLS

2 1 rise   2 melt   3 ice   4 snow   5 growing   6 75
7 1/3   8 25   9 billion   10 19

UNIT 2 LANGUAGE QUIZ
PART A KEY VOCABULARY

1 1 c   2 e   3 d   4 b   5 g   6 i   7 f   8 a   9 h

2 1 Logging   2 rainforests   3 threatened
4 global warming   5 atmosphere
6 greenhouse gases

PART B LANGUAGE DEVELOPMENT

3 1 contribute to   2 predict   3 annual   4 trend
5 challenges

4 1 plants   2 greenhouse   3 climate   4 tropical
5 environmental

UNIT 2 WRITING QUIZ
PART A GRAMMAR FOR WRITING

1 1 Destruction of forests leads to erosion and problems with the soil.
2 Climate change is the result of human behavior.
3 Flooding and changes in sea level are caused by melting glaciers.
4 Burning fossil fuels results in an increase in carbon dioxide.
5 Warmer temperatures are due to climate change.

2 1 because   2 because of   3 because of
4 because of   5 because

PART B WRITING TASK

3 *Answers will vary.*

UNIT 3 READING QUIZ
PART A KEY SKILLS

1 1 T 2 F 3 F

PART B ADDITIONAL SKILLS

2 1 Water taxis 2 Ox carts 3 bicycles 4 Public
5 railroads 6 Rickshaws 7 trains/railways

3 1, 3, 5

UNIT 3 LANGUAGE QUIZ
PART A KEY VOCABULARY

1 1 congestion 2 vehicles 3 rail 4 outskirts
5 commuters 6 practical 7 connect
8 government

2 1 c 2 a 3 d 4 e 5 f 6 b

PART B LANGUAGE DEVELOPMENT

3 1 c 2 f 3 e 4 g 5 d 6 b 7 a

4 1 traffic congestion 2 bike lane
3 public transportation 4 parking restrictions
5 road rage

5 1 convince 2 consider 3 prevent 4 require
5 attempt

UNIT 3 WRITING QUIZ
PART A GRAMMAR FOR WRITING

1 1 If we add more water taxis, we will increase traffic on the river.
2 If we reduce the number of trains, rail commuters will get angry.
3 If the city tests vehicle emissions, we will have better air.
4 If we increase the driving age, fewer young people will have accidents.
5 If the city increases the number of bike lanes, more people will cycle.

2 1 unless 2 If, not 3 Unless 4 not, unless

PART B WRITING TASK

3 *Answers will vary.*

UNIT 4 READING QUIZ
PART A KEY SKILLS

1 1 P1: From the samba in Brazil to the halay in Turkey, traditional dances are part of the culture and history of many countries. P2: No matter its origin, morris dancing is very lively. P3: Morris dances have a long tradition, but the dance also changes with the times.
2 May
3 (1) Although some people think it can be traced to the 14th century, (2) others point to its appearance in plays by Shakespeare in the 17th century. (3) Finally, it is others' belief that the name comes from the Moors of North Africa.
4 costume
5 The dancers often have bells on their knees that ring loudly as they dance. / They often wave white handkerchiefs or carry short sticks that they bang together as they dance.
6 invented

PART B ADDITIONAL SKILLS

2 1 a 2 b 3 a 4 a 5 b

UNIT 4 LANGUAGE QUIZ
PART A KEY VOCABULARY

1 1 a 2 a 3 b 4 a 5 b 6 b 7 a 8 b

2 1 relationships 2 couple 3 engaged 4 ceremony
5 cultures 6 formal

PART B LANGUAGE DEVELOPMENT

3 1 Many people in the United States love football.
2 Couples usually have receptions after their wedding ceremonies.
3 German speakers tend to be more direct than English speakers.
4 Couples occasionally expect you to fly to a vacation destination for their wedding.
5 Americans tend to dress informally.
6 The Japanese culture can be quite formal.
7 People normally give speeches and congratulate newlyweds at the reception.
8 When you visit someone's house for the first time, you are frequently expected to bring a gift.
9 In India, many people think it is impolite to say "no."
10 Couples sometimes do not have a wedding celebration with friends or relatives.

4 1 important 2 obvious 3 brief 4 common
5 certain

UNIT 4 WRITING QUIZ
PART A GRAMMAR FOR WRITING

1 I, S

2 *Possible answers:*
1 The English folk dance called "morris" originally celebrated spring.
2 Modern ideas are now included in morris dancing.
3 According to Jonathan Milton, the Wiltshire morris dance about the Great Bustard has a powerful message not seen in this lively dance before.

PART B WRITING TASK

3 *Answers will vary.*

UNIT 5 READING QUIZ
PART A KEY SKILLS

1 2, 5

PART B ADDITIONAL SKILLS

2 1 28 2 770 3 oxygen 4 blood 5 fat

UNIT 5 LANGUAGE QUIZ
PART A KEY VOCABULARY

1 1 campaigns 2 active 3 self-esteem
4 moderate 5 balanced diet 6 obesity 7 junk food 8 recognize

2 1 nutritional 2 calories 3 portion 4 reduce
5 serious

PART B LANGUAGE DEVELOPMENT

3 1 ~~recognition~~; recognize 2 ~~reduction~~; reduce
3 ~~encouragement~~; encourage
4 ~~advertise~~; advertisements / advertising
5 ~~promotion~~; promote

4 1 e 2 d 3 b 4 c 5 a

UNIT 5 WRITING QUIZ
PART A GRAMMAR FOR WRITING

1 1 In my view, children should / ought to / shouldn't eat junk food.
2 In my opinion, people should / ought to / shouldn't buy organic fruits and vegetables.
3 I think (that) people need to / don't need to / have to / don't have to exercise every day to be healthy.
4 I believe (that) it is / is not the government's job to keep people healthy.
5 In my opinion, most people get / don't get enough sleep.

2 1 so 2 to 3 so that 4 so 5 in order to

PART B WRITING TASK

3 *Answers will vary.*

UNIT 6 READING QUIZ
PART A KEY SKILLS

1 1 vacuum cleaners and lawnmowers
2 help out in the home, play sports, and dance
3 5 feet 2 inches / 158 centimeters
4 a camera
5 They can help people. / They can complete work that could be harmful to humans, assist people in need, and do some of the tasks humans do not want to do.

PART B ADDITIONAL SKILLS

2 1 T
2 F; While these robots for the home are helpful, they are nothing compared with the human-like robot ASIMO.
3 T
4 F; Researchers are improving robots so robots can learn about the world and respond to human voice and touch.
5 T

UNIT 6 LANGUAGE QUIZ
PART A KEY VOCABULARY

1 1 harmful 2 essential 3 movements 4 power
5 prevent 6 artificial 7 unlimited 8 pattern

2 1 f 2 e 3 g 4 d 5 b 6 a 7 c

PART B LANGUAGE DEVELOPMENT

3 1 will definitely 2 will probably 3 could possibly
4 probably won't 5 definitely won't

4 1 c 2 d 3 e 4 b 5 a

UNIT 6 WRITING QUIZ
PART A GRAMMAR FOR WRITING

1 1 One research study about robots involved a ten-year-old girl who was given a robot doll for several weeks.
 2 The design manager has a favorite question that/which is about what robots will be like in the future.
 3 Most people choose to use an elevator, which is a kind of machine, instead of taking the stairs.
 4 I'm sending you an email I received from Max Mustermann, who attended your webinar about robots.
 5 Please provide a short description that/which includes details of the design of your robot.

2 1 d 2 c 3 e 4 a 5 b

PART B WRITING TASK

3 *Answers will vary.*

UNIT 7 READING QUIZ
PART A KEY SKILLS

1 1 Opinion 2 Fact 3 Opinion 4 Fact
 5 Opinion

PART B ADDITIONAL SKILLS

2 a 2 b 4 c 1 d 5 e 3

UNIT 7 LANGUAGE QUIZ
PART A KEY VOCABULARY

1 1 outsource 2 manufacture 3 offshore 4 wages
 5 invested 6 volume 7 conditions

2 1 brands 2 textile 3 season 4 collections
 5 cotton 6 imports 7 multinational

PART B LANGUAGE DEVELOPMENT

3 1 c 2 a 3 d 4 b 5 e

UNIT 7 WRITING QUIZ
PART A GRAMMAR FOR WRITING

1 1 In addition 2 Along 3 Other 4 rather
 5 except 6 In spite 7 instead 8 result of
 9 Due 10 apart

PART B WRITING TASK

2 *Answers will vary.*

UNIT 8 READING QUIZ
PART A KEY SKILLS

1 2, 3, 4, 5

PART B ADDITIONAL SKILLS

2 1 elections 2 economy 3 natural resources
 4 recession 5 investments 6 sales 7 interest
 8 overseas 9 manufacturing 10 standard of living

UNIT 8 LANGUAGE QUIZ
PART A KEY VOCABULARY

1 1 h 2 f 3 a 4 e 5 d 6 b 7 g 8 c

2 1 value 2 factors 3 expenditures 4 investors
 5 investment

PART B LANGUAGE DEVELOPMENT

3 1 ~~finance~~; financial 2 ~~poverty~~; poor
 3 ~~valuable~~; value 4 ~~economic~~; economy
 5 ~~employed~~; employment

4 1 trend 2 demand 3 market 4 purchases
 5 consumers

UNIT 8 WRITING QUIZ
PART A GRAMMAR FOR WRITING

1 1 a slight rise 2 fall dramatically 3 decrease
 4 slight increase 5 gradual decrease

2 1 From 2 Between 3 of 4 and 5 to

3 1 d 2 c 3 a 4 e 5 b

PART B WRITING TASK

4 *Answers will vary.*

CREDITS

The authors and publishers acknowledge the following sources of copyright material and are grateful for the permissions granted. While every effort has been made, it has not always been possible to identify the sources of all the material used, or to trace all copyright holders. If any omissions are brought to our notice, we will be happy to include the appropriate acknowledgements on reprinting and in the next update to the digital edition, as applicable.

Photo credits
p. 55 (photo 1): Dinodia Photo/Passage/Getty Images; p. 55 (photo 2): Meinzahn/iStock Editorial/Getty Images Plus/Getty Images.

Front cover photographs by (woman) Amazingmikael/Shutterstock and (BG) romakoma/Shutterstock.

Corpus
Development of this publication has made use of the Cambridge English Corpus (CEC). The CEC is a multi-billion word computer database of contemporary spoken and written English. It includes British English, American English, and other varieties of English. It also includes the Cambridge Learner Corpus, developed in collaboration with the University of Cambridge ESOL Examinations. Cambridge University Press has built up the CEC to provide evidence about language use that helps to produce better language teaching materials

Cambridge Dictionaries
Cambridge dictionaries are the world's most widely used dictionaries for learners of English. The dictionaries are available in print and online at dictionary.cambridge.org. Copyright © Cambridge University Press, reproduced with permission.

Typeset by emc design ltd